Buying & Selling a Business

a Business

*How You Can Win
in the Business Quadrant*

GARRETT SUTTON, ESQ.

Buying & Selling a Business

a Business

How You Can Win
in the Business Quadrant

GARRETT SUTTON, ESQ.

Published by BZK Press, LLC

Rich Dad Advisors, B-I Triangle, CASHFLOW Quadrant and other Rich Dad marks are registered trademarks of CASHFLOW Technologies, Inc.

BZK Press LLC
2248 Meridian Blvd.
Suite H
Minden, NV 89423
775-782-2201
Visit our Web sites: BZKPress.com and RichDadAdvisors.com

Printed in the United States of America

First Edition: April 2003
First BZK Press Edition: June 2012

ISBN: 978-1-937832-04-9

Acknowledgments

The author would like to thank Mona Gambetta, Cindie Geddes, Brandi MacLeod and Tom Wheelwright for their assistance in reviewing and shaping this book. As well, the author would like to thank Robert Kiyosaki for his support and interest in this project.

Best-Selling Books
In the Rich Dad Advisors Series

by Blair Singer

SalesDogs
You Don't Have to Be an Attack Dog to Explode Your Income

Team Code of Honor
The Secrets of Champions in Business and in Life

by Garrett Sutton, Esq.

Start Your Own Corporation
Why the Rich Own their Own Companies and Everyone Else Works for Them

Writing Winning Business Plans
*How to Prepare a Business Plan that Investors will Want to Read –
and Invest In*

Buying and Selling a Business
How You Can Win in the Business Quadrant

The ABCs of Getting Out of Debt
Turn Bad Debt into Good Debt and Bad Credit into Good Credit

Run Your Own Corporation
*How to Legally Operate and Properly Maintain Your Company
into the Future*

The Loopholes of Real Estate
Secrets of Successful Real Estate Investing

by Ken McElroy

The ABCs of Real Estate Investing
The Secrets of Finding Hidden Profits Most Investors Miss

The ABCs of Property Management
What You Need to Know to Maximize Your Money Now

The Advanced Guide to Real Estate Investing
How to Identify the Hottest Markets and Secure the Best Deals

by Tom Wheelwright

Tax-Free Wealth
*How to Build Massive Wealth by **Permanently** Lowering Your Taxes*

Contents

Foreword
by Robert Kiyosaki

My poor dad encouraged me to get a good education so I could find a secure job working for a good business. My rich dad did not offer the same advice. Instead he said, "The richest people in the world learn to buy and sell businesses, not work for them."

It is a great pleasure to add to the Rich Dad Advisor series, this very important book. Garrett Sutton's information is priceless for anyone who wants to increase his or her knowledge of the often secret world of the rich, what the rich invest in, and some of the reasons why the rich get richer.

Years ago my rich dad taught me that there are three main asset classes investors invest in. They are businesses, paper assets, and real estate. In today's world of shaken investor confidence in the stock market, less than honest financial practices by corporate executives, insider trading, and questionable accounting practices, this book on buying and selling businesses offers investors choices beyond the tarnished world of paper assets and overpriced real estate.

Buying and selling businesses is not for the average investor. In fact, if you do now know what you are doing, buying and selling businesses can be the riskiest of all the three investment classes. At the same time, buying and selling businesses can be by far the most profitable of all the three asset classes...again if you know what you are doing. That is why this book is so important. It gives the Rich Dad Advisors series of books, a deeper look into the world of business, a depth required for any investors ready to take control of their financial future by owning businesses.

Personally I am glad I followed by rich dad's advice and decided to build, buy, and sell businesses, rather than work for them. I trust you'll find this book as beneficial to your financial education as my rich dad's advice was to me.

Robert Kiyosaki

Introduction

Congratulations. By reading this book you are going to learn the steps and strategies necessary to successfully buy and sell a business. The key word from that last sentence is "successfully," for there are many risks and challenges to master and overcome when buying and selling a business. But by applying the information you are about to gain, combined with using your professional team of advisors at the right times, you will come out of a business purchase transaction successfully and to your benefit.

So, let's get started...

Chapter One

Before You Begin

Being Your Own Boss

It sounds like paradise – being your own boss. Owning your own business, setting your own hours, answering to no one, even dressing how you like. Robert Kiyosaki's Rich Dad advocates owning businesses, ideally managed by others, for the income they generate and the freedom they can provide. But whether you are a non managing entrepreneur or a day-to-day boss, being the owner also means taking the responsibility – all the responsibility – for the business's health. The success or failure of your business (and correspondingly your personal financial success) lies squarely on your shoulders. There are no sick days, no vacation pay, no downsizing opportunities. A turn in the economy no longer means only worry over job security, but worry over utter financial ruin. There are no security blankets in the entrepreneurial world, so you'd better know from the start if you are a Linus or a Lucy. Linus was the intellectual of the Peanuts gang, but he required security. Lucy was the go-getter, schemer who never thought anything through. Somewhere between the personalities of this brother-sister duo is the ideal entrepreneur. Do you have the right entrepreneurial personality?

Before you buy a business, recognize that knowing your strengths and weaknesses going in can save you hours, possibly years, of frustration, as well as limit your financial risk. Ask yourself some questions. Here are a few with which to start:

- How does your education compare to the demands of the industry you plan to enter?

- Do you know how to track financials and plan for taxes?

- How do you feel about sales and marketing? How does your experience stack up?

- Do your skills lend themselves to running the type of business you are considering?

- Will your needs be met by your skills? If not, are these skills ones you can learn? If so, how long will it take you to get up to speed?

- On a more interior level, how do the needs of the business fit your personality? If you don't really like people, you may not enjoy retail. If you abhor math, the intense financial and money management aspects of manufacturing won't likely be to your liking.

- Some businesses live and die at the feet of a strong leader. The identity of the business may be the identity of the owner. Can you be all things to all people?

- Some businesses require travel or heavy lifting or working nights, weekends and holidays. Does your lifestyle allow for that? Are you willing to make the necessary changes? The odds of succeeding at a business you don't like, or whose demands do not naturally suit you, aren't good. Go with what you enjoy, what you know, or what you can learn.

- How do your goals measure up to what the business can realistically offer? Passion will take you far, knowledge even further, but in the end it may be the numbers that tell the tale. So don't make decisions without them. Let your passion be for your objectives, even an industry, but not a particular business. Let your heart have its say, but let your head lead the way.

- Will you be a good entrepreneur? Consider the following:

1. Do you need a lot of supervision or do you find your own way?
2. Are you trusted by others?
3. Are you responsible by choice or by force?
4. Are you a people person?
5. Are you a leader?
6. Are you willing to go the distance even if there is no immediate reward in sight?
7. Are you a decision-maker?
8. Can you put the big picture before immediate reward?
9. Do you finish what you start?

- Do you know who you are and what you want? Pull out your resume. Analyze it realistically. Write out your goals. Write out the realistic potential of the company you are considering. Imagine yourself running the company. Be specific. There is power in the specificity of written goals: Let them guide you in deciding if you are right for the business and if the business is right for you.

- How will your family adapt? Now, before any papers are signed and any obligations finalized, is the time to bring in family considerations.

1. What will the extra hours and extra worry do to your family?
2. Will family members be able or willing to help carry the load?
3. How will the decrease in financial security affect the cohesiveness of your family?
4. Is it worth giving up the concreteness of paychecks, insurance, retirement benefits, vacation and the like for the pride of ownership and the hopes of long-term payoff? In the language of Robert Kiyosaki's Cash Flow Quadrant, are you ready to go from being an E (Employee) to an S (Self-Employed Business Owner) to hopefully a B (Owner of a Business Managed by Others).
5. What is the flexibility of family members – financially, psychologically and emotionally? Make sure you know everyone's needs and consider whether this purchase will meet those needs.

6. If you don't get family support, will you be able to do it on your own? Family-run businesses don't necessarily put the whole family to work. If you expect help from a spouse, children or others, you need to get their support long before the closing.

• Are you running from something (dead-end job, mind-numbing boredom, the boss from hell) or toward something (self-esteem, independence, creativity)? If you are running from something, no business will take you far enough. But if you are running toward something, the distance will be greatly shortened with a bit of forethought and planning.

Why Buy (vs. Start Up)

Preparation and hard work can lead to personal fulfillment, a career you control and financial independence. When you're the boss, you determine how much time you put in and how much money you take out. When success does come, it is your success. Your hours lead to your income. You are not just lining someone else's pockets.

There is much less financial risk involved with buying an existing business than with starting one up. It is that initial period from startup to breaking even that is the most deadly for a business. An existing business must be doing something right to still be in existence. The rewards of ownership and independence are the same for a startup and for an existing business, but an existing business has a past to help guide the future. A path has been cleared for new owners to tread.

History is a valuable tool in any business. There is a level of expectation – a theoretical roadmap for the future. It is this aura of predictability that makes financing a purchase easier than financing a startup. The existing business has financial statements, assets, cash flow – in short, collateral that can be used for bank loans. And if the banks prove uninterested, many a motivated seller will help out with the financing, often with better terms than a commercial lender. An owner may even stick around after the sale to help with the often complicated, always delicate transition period.

We live in a time when small businesses are not only able to exist alongside big businesses; they are able to thrive. Technology has made access nearly seamless. Your business can reach customers on the other side of the world just as easily as the other side of the street. Fax, E-mail, Internet, video conferencing, printed material – all allow a local business to reach a global market while keeping overhead low and inventory small. These avenues may not have been explored by a company's current owner and could be the difference between his or her getting by and your getting ahead.

Why Sell (vs. Hang On)

The best time to sell is when the economy and the industry are in good shape. While sellers have little or no control over these factors, they can keep their companies in prime selling condition in order to take advantage of unforeseen opportunities. A well-run business is a valuable commodity in any market. Knowing economic and industry norms and how the company stacks up against them will help a seller set the best price should he or she decide to sell.

Sometimes events completely out of a seller's sphere of influence pop up and motivate a sale. Some of these include:

- Change in the competition (such as when a large company decides to move into the arena and is looking for a company to buy)

- Death of a partner or a majority shareholder (the owner may have to sell to pay off other partners or to divide up the deceased's estate)

- The owner's own heirs don't want the company (or are not competent to run it)

- Unexpected changes in finances (such as from divorce or medical emergencies)

- Changes in the rules (such as zoning changes or new laws)

Sometimes events completely within the seller's sphere of influence are prompting the sale. Sellers must understand their motivations to avoid making a mistake.

Burnout is a common sale motivator. But burnout is seldom long-term; a sale is. Maybe the seller just needs a vacation or shorter hours. Maybe he or she needs to shake things up and bring the fun and adventure back into the business. If the owner decided to sell, that freedom (just as with short-timer's syndrome in the workaday world) might prompt him or her to make changes. Sellers, why not make those changes now?

Timing

Timing is important whether buying or selling a business. The health of the overall economy, the state of the company's specific industry, and the condition of the company all play into the decision-making process. The overall economy's health may dictate the availability of loans while also coloring the perspective of potential buyers. Good economic times breed optimistic buyers. Optimistic buyers have rosier hopes for the future, and it is this future they are purchasing. The state of the target company's industry and the health of the target business help define levels of perceived risk. Lower risk means higher prices, even if those risks are only in the eye of the beholder.

While buyers and sellers have no control over the health of economy or even the state of the industry, assessing trends and perceptions will greatly influence their ability to be in the right place at the right time. The key ingredient to good luck is good planning.

Economic slumps may be good news for buyers. If buyers have the purchasing power (or better yet, the cash), there are usually bargains to be had during a recession. Of course, the risks are higher. After all, buyers are likely buying in the hopes of the economy turning around. Eventually it will, but weathering the storm can be an expensive proposition.

Economic booms may be good news for sellers. Optimism loosens purse strings. But higher purchase prices generally mean more debt for the buyer and if optimism turns out to be unfounded, carrying a company with significant debt and insufficient valuation may require a buyer to sell. A struggling company in a struggling economy is the worst of all situations for the seller.

Either way, in good economies or bad, buyers want to be sure they have enough money on hand to cover not only the purchase but also the initial slump that generally accompanies new ownership.

Risk of No Sale

Imagine putting a company up for sale and getting no offers. Or getting only low offers. What went wrong? Maybe the asking price was too high. This would be the time for the seller to go back to the value analysis and reconsider the assumptions used in projections of future sales. Were the assumptions realistic? If the owner still wants to sell, he or she will need to consider lowering the price or taking the company off the market. If the former, the seller may need an ego check first. If the latter, damage control is warranted.

A good way to understand some of the concepts we're discussing is through the use of case studies. Our first one is instructive.

Case No. 1 – Walter, Peter and Anian

Walter owned a chain of three closet design and home organizing businesses in a large, populous state. Walter did a fair amount of advertising and so many people throughout the region knew of The Closet Admiral.

Walter had built the business up to the point where he could step away and do other things. He had brought in Peter to be the general manager of the three closet design businesses. Peter, being aggressive and confident in his abilities, insisted that he be able to acquire an ownership interest in the business over time. Walter agreed to this, but beyond an acceptance in principal, the negotiations had not yet begun and the terms for an acquisition of ownership had not even been discussed.

Shortly thereafter, Walter's plans for the business changed. An opportunity to own an even more profitable business with a much greater upside potential had landed in Walter's lap. To pull it off, he would have to sell The Closet Admiral in order to generate enough cash for the down payment he needed on the new business.

Walter decided to quietly solicit offers to purchase The Closet Admiral. He wanted to fly under the radar, so that no one would know of, or impede, his future plans. He didn't tell Peter or his banker or any of his inside circle of advisors.

Anian owned a chain of five closet design locations in the southern part of the state. She was a hard-nosed businesswoman, always interested in a deal. When Walter approached her about a quiet sale she responded with interest. On a handshake, she agreed to keep the whole matter confidential. In reality, she just wanted to see Walter's books. She wanted to know how he had been able to expand so quickly.

After reviewing the books, Anian placed two disastrous phone calls. First, she called Walter's banker to demand why she couldn't get the same favorable terms that Walter had received for equipment purchases. The banker was very angry that the confidential relationship between he and Walter had been compromised. Then, Anian called Peter to see if he would work for her. Peter learned for the first time that the business he thought he had an ownership interest in was for sale. He was furious at Walter for what he considered to be an offensive betrayal of trust.

Both Peter and the banker refused to do business with Walter again. Peter quit in a very loud and derisive manner, encouraging other employees to quit as well, many of whom did. The banker called several of Walter's promissory notes, forcing Walter to scramble to find alternative financing, and killing all of Walter's hopes for completing the other business opportunity he had sought to pursue.

The disruption caused Walter to almost lose the business. When the employees left they took some of their regular referral sources with them. Some of his best employees started working at two new, very competitive closet design firms – that Anian had opened up in the area.

Walter hung on by assuring the remaining employees that they would always have a place to work, that he was not selling the business, and that their job security was as important to him as it was to them. It took almost a year, but Walter brought the business back. And he had learned a very valuable lesson about the confidentiality needed when selling a business, and the care needed in selecting the right potential buyers.

As we have just seen, company sales affect more than just buyers and sellers. Customers, vendors and employees can all find out about the possibility of a sale, and emotional reactions are inevitable. Fear of what is to come may have some already looking for new suppliers, customers and jobs. The fallout can be far-reaching without the owner ever even knowing about it. Therefore, sellers need to be proactive from the beginning. Confidentiality agreements are a must to keep the news of a sale on a need-to-know basis. The agreement should be in writing with, if possible, a damage provision for the unauthorized release of confidential information. However, this type of contractual provision will only take the seller so far. Once the others find out, or are likely about to find out (and be assured, they WILL learn of a potential sale), the seller needs to start talking and alleviating fears. And you'd better have your story consistent and down pat, because your employees are going to want to hear something that is reasonable, reassuring and makes sense.

How to Handle a Failed Sale

If the sale does not go through and the company is taken off the market, the owner will need to talk to those involved and reassure them all that he or she is recommitted to the business and looking forward to future success. Any sense of failure projected by an owner will lead others into the cycle of uncertainty. As we all know from experience, uncertainty leads to fear. Fear leads to grasping for safety. And that search for safety can mean customers, vendors and employees finding new opportunities elsewhere and leaving the owner behind.

To allay customer fears after deciding not to sell, owners should redouble customer service efforts. It is unlikely that most customers will even know there was the potential of a sale, but the owner has no way of knowing who might or might not have heard the news. Customer service never hurts a business and making service a priority not only convinces those who did hear that you are recommitted to the business but may increase loyalty of those who never even knew anything was in the offing. For those who ask what happened, be frank but don't give away details. Customers need reassurance, not a lesson in capitalism. As Henry Ford said, "Never complain, never explain."

The fallout with vendors could have financial consequences. Most vendors have relationships with owners based on long-term rewards. They may offer good credit deals in hopes of keeping an owner's business for a long time. The news of a company being up for sale makes those long-term hopes less likely. Don't expect the news of the sale not going through to be a relief. It is likely that vendors will now see the company as a short-term investment (they will be wondering if the owner is still trying to sell, questioning his or her commitment). This is especially true with smaller, privately held businesses where relationships are more intimate. Owners may find vendors have hurt feelings about being kept in the dark. While from your perspective it is none of their business, from their viewpoint it is their business. Your business is their business. Appreciating their position will help in understanding the dynamics involved.

Employees likely will be relieved the company is no longer for sale, but they may have some of the same feelings as vendors and customers. They may still question owner loyalty. Once that happens, their own levels of loyalty are likely to decrease as they turn more toward protecting themselves. Morale is likely down. Owners might consider having a company party or perhaps a team-building retreat to reinvigorate the company.

No matter what work the owner puts in, the damage may be done. In the end, there is still the danger that not selling will cost the owner more than dropping the price would have.

Rich Dad's Tips

- Know your strengths and weaknesses before buying a business.

- Be prepared to accept complete personal responsibility for the success or failure of your business.

- As a seller of a business know and understand the consequences of a failed business sale.

Let's now review the strategies of buyers and sellers ...

Chapter Two

Buyers and Sellers

Buyer Strategy/Seller Strategy

Just as with so many other things in life, it takes two to buy a business. A buyer and a seller are the key ingredients. Brokers, accountants, lawyers and other experts make sure everything is in the right measure and you don't get burned. But without a willing buyer and a motivated seller there is no deal. And they may have more in common than they think.

Both the buyer and the seller want the company sold. Both want as painless a process as possible. Both want it over quickly. Neither wants to get very far into the deal and have it fall apart. Neither wants the word to get out that the deal is in process. And neither wants the business to fail.

With so much in common, how could anything go wrong? Simple, buyers and sellers speak different languages. Each is reading for different clues, deciphering vastly different nuances, viewing the whole process through a different set of lenses. And this is exactly as it should be. Friendly skepticism is the ideal in all adversarial transactions. Former American President, Ronald Reagan, used to chide the then-Soviet Premier, Mikhail Gorbachev, with the phrase "Trust, but Verify." The United States was willing to accept what the Russians said was true only after the United States had verified it to be true. As with nuclear warheads, the same is true for deal points. While negotiations may be pleasant exchanges and the buyer and seller may become best buddies after all is said and done, neither should lose that sense of skepticism and the need to verify key points.

It goes without saying that the wants and needs of buyers and sellers are often at odds with one another. Knowing these wants and needs, being able to put yourself in the other party's shoes, will help in reaching a deal that is acceptable to both sides. Or it may just as easily assist in a deal not coming together. It should be noted that not every deal is finalized, nor should they be concluded. Some deals you will walk away from, a few you will run from. By following the key elements we discuss in this book, by using your intuition and judgment, you will know which deals to complete and which to discard as unrealistic, overpriced or downright scary.

As a general overview, the buyer is watching the road ahead. All discussions are filtered through a view of future goals. In contrast, the seller is watching the rearview mirror. All discussions are filtered through historical contexts. While both may be in the same room, they often hear different conversations due to their respective filters. Knowing this and trying to see through the other's filter can make the whole process a little more clear.

Know your audience. Both buyer and seller are auditioning. Both are posturing. The buyer wants to convince the seller that he or she has the financial and moral wherewithal to live up to contractual obligations. The seller wants to convince the buyer that his or her company is the best bargain going. It's important to remember who the audience is in order to give it what it wants. For example, if the seller is concerned about the future of employee positions and the buyer is only focusing on streamlining management, neither will be satisfied.

Case No. 2 – Paris and Richard

Paris was an up-and-coming real estate broker in an affluent area. He had attracted a following by providing excellent and expert service, as well as by being involved in every civic group in town. He was unapologetically aggressive in all of his dealings. He was working for a large national brokerage firm, but was ready to branch out on his own. Rather than build up a real-estate company from scratch, he wanted to save, in his estimation, ten years in establishing name recognition by acquiring an existing business.

Richard owned Piedmont Realty, which had three decent producing offices, thirty brokers and had been in business for over forty-five years. Richard was considering retirement but was concerned about what would happen to the other brokers in the office, whom he considered to be family. When Paris approached him about selling, he was hesitant. He was unsure if Paris was the right person to continue the family tradition of Piedmont Realty.

But Richard was encouraged by his attorney to consider Paris' expression of interest. The attorney explained that if Richard retired without selling the business his family of brokers would be disbanded anyway. It was at least worth listening to what Paris had to offer.

A contract was drawn up by Richard's attorney requiring Paris to keep the entire transaction confidential. He was not allowed to speak to any of Richard's brokers, vendors or customers about the potential purchase. Paris was allowed to review Richard's financial books and records and speak to Richard's CPA about the business. He was allowed after-hours access to the office, accompanied by Richard, and that was all. He was given two weeks to engage in a due diligence (investigative) review of Piedmont Realty. Richard didn't want to waste a lot of time and money on a transaction he didn't see working out anyway.

Eleven days later, after reviewing the relevant documents and sizing up office procedures, Paris met with Richard. The fatal posturing began. Paris started by pointing out that Piedmont Realty was not search engine optimized. No one could find Piedmont Realty on the internet, which was now a key to real estate success. Paris told Richard to bring Piedmont Realty to current information technology standards would cost $50,000. Paris then said that any purchase price they agreed upon would have to be reduced by $50,000 since that is what Paris would have to invest to get Piedmont Realty found on the internet.

Richard was offended by this opening gambit. He didn't like the way Paris was handling things, so he cut to the chase. Three key brokers had been with Piedmont Realty for a long time. Cowboy, Jimmie and Evalynn had helped him through thick and thin, and Richard wanted a guarantee that the three could remain for as long as they wanted.

Paris had crunched the numbers. On a per-desk basis, accounting for all overhead and administrative items, each broker had to bring in $3,500 per month for Piedmont Realty to break even. Only Cowboy was meeting that monthly nut. The company was losing thousands per year by having Jimmie and Evalynn, now less productive brokers, taking up desk space. Paris said they would be given six months to increase their productivity to above break-even. If they couldn't do it, their desk would be given to a more aggressive broker.

That was all Richard needed to hear. Right then and there he decided he would never sell his company to Paris. He would rather lose some money and allow the company to slowly wither away, if that was to be its fate, than to ever make (or allow someone else to make) production demands on the key employees who got him there in the first place.

For Paris' part, he moved onto the next seller. While he understood Richard's loyalty to his employees, he was a dispassionate buyer. He could never own a business where there were constraints on who he could terminate. If Richard couldn't get past his ego and emotion to conclude a sale, so be it. Paris was unemotional and would look elsewhere.

As the case illustrates, frequently the objectives of the buyer and seller are going to be very different. Better to spend a short period of time – a two-week due diligence review – and see if the differences are too large to overcome, than spend months and months of time before getting to the central issues motivating the buyer and seller. This strategy allowed Paris to get to the heart of the matter and move on. It also saved both Paris and Richard from the high legal fees that can add up in the sale of a business. Understanding and overcoming each party's objectives early on can help lead to a successful sale. The longer key objectives are left unaddressed, the more likely they will be left to explode at the end, thus potentially derailing any sale and wasting a lot of time and money in the process.

The Seller

As a seller, you are looking for a buyer. Ideally, you want to find a buyer who does not compete for your ongoing business, presents the least hassle after the sale and offers you top dollar. Since there is a chance you may end up working for him or her after the sale, during the transition period, you will also need to evaluate if he or she is someone with whom you can work.

Keep your ego out of the sale. Every buyer will find flaws with your company – that's the buyer's job. A new buyer needs to know how to improve the business. He or she will want to do things differently than you to make the business more successful. Don't take it personally.

In our last case, Paris wanted a $50,000 reduction for a lack of information technology infrastructure. This offended Richard, whose ego and identity were intertwined with the business. A more dispassionate seller may have resolved to increase their bottom line selling price by $100,000 to cover the asked-for $50,000 reduction, and privately punish the buyer another $50,000 for even making such a reduction demand. Remember, he who cares least wins.

The sooner you can let go of your personal feelings about the business, the sooner real negotiations can begin, and the sooner you can win. Ideally, you should be letting go before the sale even gets under way. After all, the best deal for the company is not always the best deal for your ego. Separate the two and you'll stand a much better chance of winning.

Remember that the buyer is looking to the future and the seller to the past. As a seller, you can use your hindsight to help the buyer see how rosy the future can be. The rosier the past, the rosier the future. Good, current, thorough books go a long way toward the fertile fields of a profitable sale.

You need to be able to not only understand what makes your company a viable purchase, but also how to present it in such a way that others can see its benefits as well. Of course, all financials should be clear and current, but other documents, such as updated policy manuals, will help as well. You should formalize all company policies and procedures. The more you have in writing the easier it will be to overcome the objections of the buyer (or worse yet, the buyer's attorney) that the company has no substance. If you know you're going to sell your business in two years but haven't got around to "getting everything down", do so immediately. You want age on the documents. The fact that they were prepared one month prior to negotiations for a sale may be used against you.

Some useful documents include:

- Company policy manual for employees. Vacation policy, sick leave, overtime, insurance, dress code - all these should be written down. (But be careful not to create a contract of employment with your employees which can later form the basis for employee litigation. Work with your attorney to draft the policy manual in a favorable manner to your company).

- Work procedures manual - detailed, step-by-step instructions on how various tasks are performed.

- Customer agreements. Get it in writing. A good, standardized agreement can save everyone from many headaches, including you. If there are issues involving performance, a good contract will provide a roadmap on how to move forward.

- Current bylaws and articles of incorporation filed with the state.

- Minutes for every major corporate decision.

- Current corporate handbook with minutes from required meetings of both directors and shareholders. (See my book "Start Your Own Corporation" on the importance of corporate minutes.)

- Current registered agent information.

- All tax returns.

Make sure all documents, especially manuals and policies, are current. Discrepancies between what you say and what you do could lead to perceptions of integrity problems. Such perceptions can muddy the waters for the rest of the purchase process.

It is best to be forthcoming with all the facts as you know them. If you have doubts about disclosing something, disclose it. Sellers are never sued for telling too much, only for not telling enough. Lawyers love bringing cases involving misrepresentations on the sale of a business. Look at it from their perspective. They've got you as a seller, who has complete information about the business. They've got their client, the buyer, who is a complete innocent, knows nothing about your business but is willing to pay you millions of dollars, based on your representations. Because you, the seller, are about to receive millions of dollars from the buyer, you owe that buyer an ethical and moral duty to disclose everything, warts and all. And if you don't, if you fail to disclose one little thing, that lawyer is going to paint you as a corrupt and unethical executive, the kind of one-dimensional businessman villain you see on poorly-written television shows, out to take advantage at every turn of innocent and good people everywhere. And guess what? The jury in your case will eat up this portrayal, as they always do, and you'll lose. The lesson here is to disclose everything.

The Buyer

Buyers analyze sellers, industries and the business up for sale. Buying a business takes preparation, knowledge and a little bit of faith. The better job you do at the first two, the easier the third becomes. And while you are doing all this preparation work and gaining all this knowledge, keep in mind that the acquisition process may take upwards of six months. In some cases, depending on market conditions, team readiness and overall complexity of the deal, it may take several years to close the sale. Don't quit your day job just yet. In fact, even after all the paperwork is signed and the sale is final, it may be prudent to work both jobs, if feasible, until the income from your new venture can replace that of your old. If double-duty is not feasible (for example, if the hours conflict), make sure you are in a financial position to take such a loss-of-income hit.

If you are not an expert in the industry you are considering entering, become one. Or at least try. Take some classes, read extensively, ask questions of people in the field, maybe even take a temporary job in that field – take the time necessary to come up to speed before the close. Being a new owner of a business is a lot like becoming a new parent. Once you finally have your baby, you won't have time for anything else – including reading parenting books. You'd best know how to deal with middle-of-the-night emergencies long before they occur.

If you are an expert in your industry, but don't have much knowledge of actual business practices, consider taking a few business courses – business law, accounting and marketing are a few must-haves. Local colleges and universities are a great resource, but they are not the only ones. Check with the Small Business Administration to see if there is a Small Business Development Center (SBDC) near you. You can access their website at www.sba.gov. SBDCs offer free courses, technical assistance and counseling including excellent help from the Service Corps of Retired Executives (or SCORE), who have their own website, at www.score.org. Also under the auspices of the SBA are Business Information Centers offering free access to the latest in high-tech hardware, software and telecommunications help, as well as training and access to research tools. Your local or state department of economic development may have information and training available as well. Take advantage of these resources. They are there to be used.

Don't underestimate the value of a mentor. Search your network of friends and family for someone who has found success in the field you want to enter. Then don't be afraid to ask for help. Most of us don't mind being considered an expert (it validates that part of us that believes we know everything) and are flattered to be asked. You'll be surprised how many business people are willing to help an honest and open person who is just starting out.

Business has its own karma in the form of contacts and favors. Networking is the heart of business. Start talking to people you trust and admire about your plans before you sign anything. Let those with more experience guide you. As your business becomes successful, you will be in the position to return the favor. Favors keep businesses running. And being able to help out the right person at the right time adds to the enjoyment of running a business.

Buying a company has more than just financial liability. You are hooking all your horses to the wagon. Your reputation, your personal finances, your family's future and your personnel are all going to be connected to this new venture. Be sure you have a strategic plan in place before you even begin to look for a company to buy. Some things to consider are:

- Why do you want to purchase a company?

- What can you do to improve your current situation instead of buying a company?

- If expanding or supplementing a current company, how would this purchase affect the current company?

- What finances or financial strategies do you have available for the purchase?

- Do you (or will you) have the time and money to take on this venture?

Once you start evaluating companies, consider the following:

- Is the company in a place you want to live?

- What are the trends in the industry?

- Will the company's reputation hurt or help your own?

- What can you do to improve the company?

- What is unique to the company?

- What personnel would you want to retain from the company after the sale?

- Is the company moving in a direction that suits you?

Once you narrow down the field to a few target companies, you can start more in-depth analyses and valuation. But remember to double-check all facts yourself. Never take the seller's word. The due diligence phase of the purchase is time-consuming and expensive, but absolutely necessary. Trust, but verify.

Win/Win

When negotiating the deal it is easy to develop tunnel vision. Dollar signs can distort anyone's view. Beware. While numbers are important (as a seller, you should make enough on the deal to at least cover your costs; as a buyer, you need to be sure you don't overextend yourself), there is more to the deal than money.

A deal must work in reality as well as on paper. The repercussions of a sale that doesn't work out can be far-reaching and long lasting.

Case No. 3 – John and Jeff

John owned a profitable plumbing business, John's Plumbing & Drain. It had been in business for over twenty years and had a good reputation in town. They weren't the cheapest plumbers in town, but their service was excellent. John knew that a large segment of the market would pay a little more for great service.

John was thinking of retiring and to test the waters, he allowed a business broker to present him with offers of inquiry. Everything had to remain confidential. John did not want any of his employees, especially his top-notch journeymen plumbers, to learn of any sale until the time was right.

The broker brought Jeff's offer to John in a matter of days. Jeff had apprenticed as a plumber and found his way into home construction. He had made some money building specialty homes, but given the inherent ups and downs of home construction, Jeff now wanted to buy a steady trade business he could manage and profit from for the next twenty years.

John agreed to meet with Jeff to discuss how the deal could come together. It was tentatively agreed that Jeff would pay $1 million for the business. Jeff would put $500,000 down and John would carry a note at

10% for the remaining $500,000, for a period of seven years. This would give John a payment of over $8,000 a month for the next seven years of his retirement. If Jeff ever defaulted on a payment, John had the right to accelerate the note and demand full payment. If Jeff couldn't refinance the note or somehow pay in full upon an acceleration demand, then John would get the business back.

The more John met with Jeff the more he realized that Jeff did not have the actual hands-on experience to run a day-to-day service driven business. As a spec builder, Jeff needed to co-ordinate various subcontractors and make sure the brokers sold the homes in time. His was not an intensive customer service business. John became concerned by some of the comments Jeff made about treating employees. He did not appear to have a common touch but rather a roughshod "my way or the highway" approach. John knew that this style may work with subcontractors, but it would not work with journeymen plumbers. A good plumber made the company good money and they weren't easily replaced. You needed to go an extra mile or two to keep them happy and to keep your profits up.

John recalled how a friend of his, looking to retire, had sold his HVAC (heating, ventilation and air conditioning) business to an entrepreneur who didn't know how to handle tradesmen. Like this deal, his friend had taken a down payment and carried a note for the balance. And what happened? The entrepreneur alienated all the top HVAC talent in the company and within several months they had all found jobs with other HVAC providers in the area. With his talent gone, the company faltered, service went down, negative word of mouth was almost instantaneous and the entrepreneur defaulted on his payments to the former owner. And so, his friend had to come back in and take over a once-solid business that had been wrecked in just six months time, due to poor management. His friend spent the rest of his life trying to rebuild the company again so that he could sell it. He died at his desk.

John did not want such a fate. He understood that if the sale wasn't a win/win on both sides, then no-one would win. He could clearly see that Jeff was out of his league in running a plumbing business. Jeff clearly would not win, which meant that John would not win. Down the line,

John knew he would have to come back in to the business and deal with the wreckage of his once-profitable company.

John told the business broker to cease any further negotiations. Jeff was furious. He claimed bad faith and threatened to sue, and never appreciated what a huge favor John had done him.

The only good deal is one that is safe for both parties. So while you are negotiating for your best deal, keep in mind the reality of the other party's situation. And this is certainly one case where the seller should take the lead. With his or her experience comes an in-depth understanding of the business. With that understanding comes tools to evaluate the safety of the deal for both parties. As communication and negotiations continue, buyer and seller should build a rapport that lends itself to trust. This is necessary for the buyer to be able to comfortably accept the counsel of the seller regarding the safety of the deal. However, this trust should not interfere with healthy skepticism. As a buyer, you need to double-check every piece of data you can. But as well, you need to listen to what the seller is telling you. It may be direct or it may be in the form of offhand or indirect comments, which may be very indicative of the seller's true feelings. Be it direct or indirect, listen for the seller's clues. He may be under pressure from a spouse or business associate to sell, but he may let you know in so many little ways that you are not the right buyer, or his is not the right business for you.

Trust is important in any negotiation, but it is absolutely necessary to the process of win/win discussions. Both parties must feel free to offer suggestions and pursue safe outcomes. However, even in situations where trust is established, conversations may turn heated. In such cases, simply take a break from controversial items and leave them for later when cooler heads can prevail. Remember that the goal is to reach the safest deal, not just the one that brings you the most dollar signs.

Listening

We have just touched on the importance of listening and it bears repeating.

An old adage says that the Almighty gave us two ears and only one mouth so that we might listen twice as much as we speak. This is great advice for the process of buying or selling a business. Both sides should be listening for deal breakers and bedrock motivations. Ask the direct questions, but also listen for indirect answers.

As a buyer, listen to why the seller is interested in getting rid of the business. Is he or she just trying to get out from under a financial burden? Is he or she unsatisfied with returns? Maybe the seller simply wants to retire or is facing medical problems that preclude running the business. Or maybe he or she has inherited partners he or she doesn't want. Any of these are fine reasons and you should feel comfortable with them. However, beware of hidden knowledge. Does the seller know about something coming that will hurt the business – competition moving in, a change in technology that could lead to obsolescence, or new patents about to be issued? Ask. Be blunt; be nosy; listen carefully to the reasons offered by the buyer. Weigh those against everything else you know about this person. If you have doubts, get in writing that withholding information that could affect the future profitability of the company is a breach of the agreement and requires a refund of all money received for purchase of the company. That should send some fur flying. It may also get you the information you need.

Trust/Intuition

Trust during negotiations is crucial. But trust isn't something you just throw out on the table. Trust is earned. By double-checking facts, a buyer learns to trust a seller and a seller learns to trust a buyer. As the sale process continues, both will reach a level of comfort with the trustworthiness of the other. If you never trust the person across the table, walk away. If you can't trust your opponent during the process, you won't be able to trust him or her to follow through with contractual agreements either. Do the legwork, follow your intuition and never be afraid to walk away. Again, he who cares least wins. If your intuition tells you it isn't right, get up and walk away without regret or remorse. You've lived to fight another day.

Rich Dad's Tips

- Put yourself in the other party's shoes. Know what they want and need out of the deal.

- Get to the central issues of the sale in short order. It will save everyone time and money in the long run.

- As a seller, have your documents in perfect order for the buyer's inevitable due diligence review.

And when it comes to trust, you are going to need to trust your team of advisors ...

Chapter Three

Your Team of Experts

Assembling Your Team

Buying a business is a risky proposition under the best of circumstances. Attempting to go it alone is the worst of circumstances. Unless you are truly an expert you will want to assemble a team of professionals to help you find your way through the legal and tax pitfalls that might be waiting around any given corner. Not only will your team scout out the lay of the land for you, they may also hook you up with contacts and pass on some of their knowledge while helping you to maintain a professional air. Lenders, buyers and sellers all pay attention to the stability and management skills of opponents in sales. Weakness, even perceived weakness, can kill your deal. You must at least appear to be an expert, and the easiest way to achieve that appearance (short of actually being an expert) is to surround yourself with knowledge. As Robert Kiyosaki's Rich Dad advised him, business and investing are team sports. Put together a winning team of advisors and you stand a much better chance of winning.

Before discussing how to assemble your team of experts, it is important to understand why so many professionals (especially attorneys) are considered deal killers when it comes to the sale of a business.

Case No. 4 – Kent and Hank

Kent and Hank had been friends since high school. They both went away to college and grad school and moved back to town to start their careers.

Kent had obtained an electrical engineering degree and then an MBA, and inherited his father's electronics repair business. He quickly expanded the business into electronic component manufacturing, both in the United States and abroad. Under Kent's more aggressive leadership, the company really started to take off.

Hank had obtained his law degree and had gone to work for a large law firm in town. Kent's company was the first new client he brought into the firm. In four years, instead of the normal seven year associate track, Hank had become a partner due solely to the fact that Kent's company provided so much work for the firm.

Kent was becoming known in the region as a leading entrepreneur. He had been selected Businessman of the Year by his state's Industrial and Economic Authority. He had been written up as a genius in Forbes, Business Week and the Wall Street Journal. Unfortunately, he started believing his own press.

Kent and Hank spent a great deal of time together. Kent was expanding into new markets, thinking about going public, and all the while getting Hank's sound legal advice for his next move. Kent was demanding of Hank's time. He needed him 24/7. And Hank gave his time to Kent out of loyalty and friendship, which was more important to him than billable hours.

Kent started thinking about acquiring an established company in a somewhat unrelated field. Time and time again Kent had to spend big dollars to get injection molds prepared for his electronic components. It was so expensive and frustrating for him that he decided to acquire his own injection molding company. Hank had urged caution, but Kent wanted to move forward.

Kent located a target company in southern Illinois. It had an excellent business track record and a good reputation in the industry. Importantly for Kent, his company could get its injection molds for 60% less than they had previously been paying.

Hank was assigned to do the due diligence investigation. All the documents, financials and procedures were in order. Everything appeared to be on the up-and-up. Still, Hank's intuition told him something wasn't right. He discussed his vague concerns with Kent over dinner. Kent dismissed his feelings as the inbred deal-killer instincts of a lawyer. Kent assured him that everything was fine.

The transaction closed. And within four months, Kent was furious at Hank for ever letting him do the deal. A number of Taiwanese injection molding companies had suddenly sprung up. They were undercutting U.S. prices by up to thirty percent. No one had seen it coming. The former owner said he knew nothing about it, and there was no evidence to prove otherwise. (Had there been, Kent would have sued in an instant).

The injection molding fiasco was a major financial and business embarrassment for Kent's company. It indefinitely put off its plans to go public. It challenged Kent's status and position as a genius entrepreneur. Kent couldn't live with this. His press clippings had said otherwise. It wasn't, it couldn't be his fault.

Who was responsible for doing the due diligence investigation? As part of that process, as part of knowing of competitive threats to the industry, who should have known that the Taiwanese were mounting an imminent and major attack on the injection molding market? There was one answer – Hank. Kent has his company's PR flacks and spin-meisters put out the word that the whole disaster was Hank's fault. Kent was led astray by Hank's advice. Kent was still the genius. Hank was now forevermore the goat.

Hank was bitterly offended by the actions of his former friend. The competitive analysis was supposed to have been done by the company's people. While it wasn't in writing, Hank had even warned Kent against the deal. And now, to be turned on like this, was something beyond belief.

It got worse. His large firm couldn't have the taint of the injection molding fiasco on their doorstep. Despite the fact that Hank's work had lined all of their pockets with tens of thousands of dollars every year for the last eight years, Hank was told to leave the firm. For his former partners, appearance was more important than reality, rejection easier than loyalty.

The lesson of this case – and be assured it has happened thousands of times around the world – is that attorneys are deal killers because of the position that they are in. For Hank, there was no upside on the deal. He would collect his fees, sure, but he would be entitled to them anyway. But if the deal was a huge success, Hank would not get the credit or a bonus, or any other benefit. Success was expected.

At the same time, Hank had all of the downside risk. If critical information wasn't ferreted out in time, if the deal didn't work for a myriad of technical reasons, the lawyer was to blame. Hank's position in the whole transaction was that of scapegoat-in-waiting.

And so, for many attorneys, it is easier to kill a deal than make one, for in killing it, no mistakes are made. There are no future problems or issues, for which scapegoats are needed.

While it is justifiable to criticize a small and select number of attorneys for their officiousness, incivility and questionable ethics, it is important to know that the syndrome of the deal-killing attorney most frequently arises outside the context of the attorney's own personality. Instead, it should be recognized that almost every attorney you will ever deal with will have had a person like Kent in his past – a client and a friend, who the attorney went all out for, only to have that person turn on them when it became convenient to do so. With most attorneys having one or more such experiences, it is no wonder that they are skeptical, resistant and on their guard in the sale of a business. Their clients, the public at large, have put them in that position.

The point of this discussion is not to create sympathy for the legal profession. Shakespeare, Twain, Hemingway, the world's most talented writers, could not do that. Rather, the point here is to help you win when you buy and sell a business. To do so, you need to know why attorneys are deal-killers. And, armed with this understanding, you can overcome the resistance of the deal-killers to your ultimate advantage.

Entering into a business purchase transaction, assume that every attorney involved in the deal is a deal-killer. They don't want to make a mistake for which they will be blamed – or sued for malpractice – at a later date. How can you win with such people at the table?

1. Be forthright. Don't hide anything. Attorneys have trained antennae that sense out when even the smallest of details don't add up. If you are evasive or furtive or, on the other hand, too slick or glib, the

attorney will be processing those impressions and recording them as a strike against you. Be honest, open and direct. It's not hard to do.

2. Focus on win/win. As we've discussed, the only good deal is one that works for both parties. Appreciate what the other side needs to get out of the deal, and openly discuss your understanding of their position. This may seem counter-intuitive to certain hard charging executives who are determined not to leave one scrap on the table for anyone else. But again, you are in a room full of deal-killers. And honey gets you more than vinegar. By tenaciously and unreasonably fighting for every last dollar, you are geometrically increasing your chances that one of the attorneys will decide that you are a future problem waiting to happen. And we know how attorneys deal with the specter of future problems. Avoidance. No deal.

3. Immaculate documents. You should see the look on some attorneys' faces when a perfectly assembled due diligence package arrives for review. You would think they'd want to start dancing. If your corporate documents – your articles, bylaws, minutes, major contracts, policy manuals, procedure manuals and the like – are in perfect order when they are shipped off to the other side's attorneys for review, you will have taken a huge step in overcoming resistance.

   Immaculate documents and documentation of corporate operations and affairs creates an extremely favorable impression. And remember that we are dealing in a certain measure here with the importance of impressions and intuition. If your documents are in precise order, it bespeaks that your organization, your means and your manner of doing business are in order as well. It gives the attorney comfort that he is not letting his client make a mistake.

   On the other hand, poor corporate records are probably the number one reason attorneys will kill a deal. You hear the lament all the time: "Their records are a mess. How can you trust them for anything?"

All right. Having discussed how to deal with deal-killers, let's explore how to assemble your team of deal advisors.

A professional team working behind the scenes can make all the difference between a good sale and a bad one. But the difference may well lie in the quality of your team. True experts don't come cheap and this is one case where it is likely you will get what you pay for. But don't let high hourly rates or fancy titles intimidate you. You are in charge. You must decide when to engage counsel, when to delegate authority and when to make your own decisions. You also need to know how to choose your team. Following are a few guidelines to use when assembling your experts.

1. First look for personal recommendations. Check with others who have bought similar businesses and ask how they felt about members of their team. Tap the knowledge of friends, relatives and business acquaintances. If you can't find any personal recommendations, check with professional associations.

2. Make a list of at least three candidates for each spot on your team.

3. Conduct interviews with each of the candidates. Don't settle for a phone interview; do it in person. You need to know if you are comfortable working with this person. If any say they are too busy or can't meet in person, consider this a big red flag and mark them off your list. Be sure to ask if they offer a free initial half-hour consultation. It never hurts to ask.

4. The interview:

*   At the interview, pay attention to how the expert treats his or her staff. Is his or her style of teamwork conducive to your own?

*   Look around the office. Is it organized? Do you see certificates from professional associations or awards from peer groups?

*   Ask about experience and education. How many similar clients has he or she had? How long has he or she been in the profession? Does this professional engage in continuing education? How does he or she stay current on changes in the field?

- Discuss your own expectations and don't be afraid to ask questions. You're not supposed to know everything; that's why you're looking for experts. However, don't shy away from a candidate who admits he or she doesn't know an answer to a question if he or she says so and promises to find out the answer. That kind of honesty can signal a keeper.

- Listen not only to the content of the candidate's answers, but also his or her conversational style. Is he or she specific or vague? Does he or she seem sincerely interested in your business plan or just your wallet? Do you trust this person?

- Get at least three client references (ask for the three most recent whose cases are similar to yours) and be sure to call them. Recognize that for attorney/client privacy purposes some lawyers won't give out references. If an attorney won't give you references, you can always go to www.lawyers.com and size up that attorney's list of representative clients.

- We're all taught it's tacky to talk about money, and most of us hate this part of the interview process, but you have to ask. Make it the last topic of conversation, but do ask. If the fee seems excessive, don't attack or criticize, simply try to negotiate. If he or she won't lower the price, there are other ways to decrease what you pay. Offer to do some of the legwork on your own. Ask about payments. Discuss whether the candidate can keep the hours lean. A little posturing on fees can be a good thing. But don't go overboard on the money issue. Remember, the professional is sizing you up, too. If he or she feels that money is going to be an issue, if they sense there's a good chance that collecting from you will be difficult, they will decline to take you as a client.

5. Once you have chosen a professional, get the agreement in writing. You want an engagement letter that sets out exactly what the expert will be doing for you and for how much. Always include how the relationship can be terminated.

What follows are specific tips on many different types of professionals you may want to engage. Few of you will need them all. In the initial stages, an accountant and attorney will do fine. But don't forget to listen to other experts as well – people whose business knowledge and integrity you trust. Ask them to look at what you're doing and tell you what they think. Sometimes those without a vested interest in the deal can offer the most clear-sighted and useful advice.

Attorney

A good attorney should be the first recruit for a buyer's team. He or she will be intimately involved with every step of the buying process and you best be comfortable with that. You should have a personal rapport with your lawyer, a trust and respect that is reciprocated. Bringing your attorney on early in the game can save you costly mistakes. Small mistakes in the beginning of a venture can snowball out of control by the closing. An experienced lawyer can help you craft a strategy and guide you through the complicated process of business purchase. He or she may even be able to lead you to business opportunities.

This is not the time for generalists. Be sure your lawyer specializes in business sales and/or acquisitions and has an understanding of tax law (better yet, have an experienced tax attorney on your team as well as one familiar with business sales and acquisitions). While he or she may have gaps in expertise (business purchases/sales are complicated legal endeavors encompassing a variety of fields of law), they should be able to put you in contact with others who can fill those gaps. A lawyer whom you can trust and with whom you can comfortably communicate is the ideal.

One of the first documents to be prepared by your lawyer will be the letter of intent. This document outlines the buyer's intention, but not legally binding obligation, to buy and the seller's non-binding obligation to sell. The legally binding part of the document deals with confidentiality and competition. The buyer cannot disclose what he or she uncovers during investigation of the business. Nor can he or she use the letter to try and get a better a deal elsewhere. The letter of intent is the document that gets the whole transaction underway.

Once the letter of intent is signed, your attorney should begin the legal investigation of the business in question. If you are looking to buy (and remember, at this point you are only looking; no commitments have been made), your lawyer will check with the secretary of state or county clerk's office (whichever is appropriate for the given jurisdiction) for any UCC-1 filings against the business. UCC-1 forms are filed by a lender when a loan is made and security interest in any assets is taken back. The form describes any assets in which the lender has an interest. You want to know if anyone has a primary interest in assets you are considering buying. Your lawyer can set up an escrow fund to cover potential claims.

Your attorney (or you, if you're on a budget and know how to do it) will also check with the county clerk's office for any liens against real estate and review zoning and business license and permit requirements. He or she will also assess any leases to be sure they are valid and can be transferred to you, as well as checking the status of any intellectual property or other proprietary information. He or she will review any lawsuits pending against the company. He or she can protect you from the former owner's creditors. If you are considering a stock transfer rather than a purchase of assets, your lawyer should review the company's bylaws, articles of incorporation, corporate minutes and stock transfer ledger to make sure the corporation you're getting is clean.

A good attorney can also draft a non-compete provision to keep the seller from competing with your new acquisition. And he or she can ensure that the seller guarantees all statements regarding liabilities, creditors and accounts receivable.

Your attorney should also be in contact with the other side's lawyer. When the deal has progressed, it is generally the buyer's lawyer who prepares the purchase agreement. Some buyers and sellers let their lawyers do the negotiations. There are pros and cons to this approach, as will be discussed later.

The final terms of purchase will be set with the help of your lawyer. And he or she will set up conditions so that once the agreement is signed, the seller will continue business as usual in order to aid a smooth transition for you, customers, creditors, employees and suppliers.

The attorney is your source for legal advice (at a cost ranging from $150 to sometimes over $400 per hour). But your attorney should not be making business decisions for you. In fact, unless he or she is an experienced businessperson, they won't likely be qualified to give you business advice. Know always that legal advice does not always constitute good business advice. For example, given the potential for product liability claims, who would ever bring a new product to market? Certainly not the lawyers. Thankfully, the market does not operate that way. Society would surely suffer and stagnate if all decisions were based solely on legal advice. No one would take a risk on anything. Indeed, some entrepreneurs seem to pay for high-priced legal advice so that they can gleefully ignore it and go with their gut. And so it is important for you to appreciate the difference between business and legal advice – that legal advice supplements and supports good business advice, and not vice-versa. In this realm, don't ever let the tail wag the dog.

A frequently asked question has to do with when should the lawyer be contacted. There is no one set or standard answer. Some will contact a lawyer at the letter of intent stage, others when it is time to prepare a buy/sell agreement. But you may need a lawyer before those thresholds. The important point to remember is that when you sense that you are getting in over your head, or just that you need independent and reasoned advice, it may be time to contact an attorney. At whatever point that is, don't be afraid to do so.

Accountant

Just as with an attorney, a good accountant is indispensable in a business-buying venture and should be brought in as early in the process as possible. Look for enthusiastic recommendations from others in your business. Ask how much of the accountant's business is with companies within your target industry. Someone who may be good with service companies may not be the same with manufacturing companies. He or she should also be able to explain complex issues in simple terms to help you make informed decisions.

Though they may charge more, a Certified Public Accountant is often the way to go. Fees can range from $150 to $350 an hour, but CPAs have a level of education and accountability (a college degree, strenuous state exams and continuing education are necessary) considered attractive to investors and bankers.

Your accountant may also be able to help you with money-raising efforts. At first, you might think this is because they know bankers. Yes, they do. But that's not their only in with money. An accountant can sometimes help with raising money through contacts with other clients as well. But don't expect them to promote this service. If they like the deal, let them offer it to you.

Your accountant will analyze the company's financials to develop an accurate picture of cash flow, expenses, revenues, profits, liabilities and assets. He or she can also assist you with future projections to show to investors and bankers. Everything from budgets to cash flow reports will be prepared by your accountant. They will also help you determine the accuracy of financial statements.

As a buyer, you are best served by bringing in your accountant to help you with strategy before you even begin to search for a business to purchase. The advance planning and financial strategies they can offer may save you from some initial missteps. As with an attorney, remember that your accountant is there to give you accurate information, to give you advice and help with strategy, but the decisions are yours to make.

Business Broker

Business brokers (also referred to as business intermediaries, or mergers and acquisitions specialists) act in the same way that real estate brokers do – as intermediaries between buyers and sellers. They have listings from numerous sellers and can search out the right business for a buyer, often working with other brokers and going through their listings as well. They may be retained by either buyer or seller (though it is usually by the seller) and are particularly useful for buyers looking for a business outside the industry with which they are familiar. Keep in mind that there are few or no requirements for business brokers. In many states anyone can become one with no experience or education. For this reason, it is very important that for buyer or seller to do some research. Referrals from lawyers, accountants or bankers are a good place to start when searching for a good business broker.

For a seller, the primary benefit of using a broker is confidentiality. The broker can field calls and deal with prospective buyers for you, thus keeping your plans for a sale away from customers, suppliers and employees. He or she can prescreen potential buyers to be sure of their level of interest as well as their ability to pay, thus saving you the hassle of dealing with looky-lous and possibly even competitors. An experienced broker can advise you how much you might be able to receive for your company and can help structure the deal in a way that minimizes your risk should the deal fall through.

A business broker charges anywhere from five 5 percent to 15 percent of the selling price, payable once the deal is done. For this reason, beware of a broker who is pushing for a close before both sides are comfortable doing so. It is not unheard of for an unscrupulous broker to push individuals to buy a business, any business, just so he or she can get the commission. It is also not unheard of for a broker to aid the seller in pumping up the sale price in order to pump up his or her own commission. So be keenly aware of what it is that gives the broker an incentive, and then stick to a strategy that is best for you.

The commission is usually paid by the seller. Sellers should try to structure the agreement so that they pay a portion at the close and the rest as the balance of the purchase price is paid. The seller should want the broker to take a risk on non-payment by the buyer as well.

Some things to consider when looking for a broker are:

- how long he or she has been in business
- what, if any, continuing education courses the broker has passed
- whether or not he or she has ever owned a business
- how many deals similar to yours he or she has brokered
- whether or not he or she (or the firm) belongs to a national broker organization (such as the International Business Brokers Association or the Institute of Certified Business Counselors)

Be sure to get references and follow through by calling them. It's also a good idea to ask each reference if they know others who have worked with the broker. Don't leave without fully understanding what the broker will do for you and then get it in writing.

Good brokers will not only ask how much a buyer has to spend, but also about professional and personal interests, as well as family and work obligations. This helps them determine what kind of business might work best for the buyer. If they show no interest in your personal life and other outside influences, consider finding a more thorough broker.

Some brokers want to do your negotiating, some don't. Regardless of what the broker wants, it is your decision on how to handle the transaction. You need to communicate your wishes clearly.

Nevertheless, buyers should consider accepting any help a broker can provide. A good one can give you information on the company's industry, market, management and customers. There is no guarantee as to the accuracy of this information, but it will be a good starting point for your own investigation. Have the broker cite his or her sources so you can go back and check the information. This will be much quicker than initially researching it yourself.

If you are a real hands-on type of person, a broker may not be for you. Brokers tend to worry about being cut out of the deal and left without a commission. Many are reluctant, at best (unwilling, at worst), to let buyers meet directly with the owner of the business, especially in the early stages of the deal. Most brokers will require sellers to sign an exclusivity agreement that says no one else has the right to sell the business during the time period spelled out in the agreement (usually at least three months). If the buyer or seller violates the agreement and/or decides not to complete the transaction, they will still have to pay that broker a commission. However, sellers can and should consider structuring the agreement so that they don't pay a commission should they sell a business to someone they find on their own.

Other Professionals

Most small business owners will use additional professionals at one time or another. These professionals may include insurance brokers, marketing consultants, advertising and public relations experts, real estate brokers and architects/designers/contractors.

Insurance brokers help to make sure a business is neither under- nor over-insured. Either case can be from significant to devastating for an entrepreneur. Be sure you are using a broker, not a salesperson, and one who is an expert at business-related policies and experienced in insuring a variety of businesses. The insurance broker can check out the business plan and know what sorts of insurance you will need, as well as how much. In some cases involving larger businesses, you will want to use a risk management consultant to analyze the risks associated with the business and suggest the appropriate level of coverage for each risk.

From worker's compensation to disability, life to fire and on and on, business insurance needs can be staggering. Don't try to figure it out on your own. You don't want to find out you are inadequately covered in the middle of a crisis. Nor do you want to be paying premiums for coverage you don't need.

Marketing consultants can help research market potential for a target business and can be useful if your own search has only made you more uncertain. Of course, you will want to be sure that the consultant has experience in the industry into which you are considering moving.

Advertising and public relations experts are valuable for the transition and the early stages of your new business venture. First impressions, you know. Make sure yours is a good one. Remember that a sale of a business is a newsworthy event for which a public relations expert may be useful.

Real estate brokers come into the game once you have decided to purchase a specific company. They can help you analyze location for suitability, growth potential and market rates for rent. They are especially valuable if you are purchasing a company in an area unfamiliar to you.

Architects, designers and contractors are needed if you are considering an expansion or renovation on the business' existing space. You'll need to have an analysis of costs and feasibility before making an offer.

All of the experts mentioned above will have a spot on your roster. You are both the coach and owner of the team. Never be afraid to surround yourself with truly talented experts. And never forget that the final calls are yours. Always let your experts support you. Never let them supplant you. With these strategies in mind, call in the right expert and the right time and you'll make the winning moves.

Rich Dad's Tips

- Understand why attorneys are deal killers and deal with them in ways to overcome such prejudices.

- Be sure to interview and get comfortable with your team of experts.

- Never forget that while experts offer advice the final decisions are yours.

Now let's get confidential ...

Chapter Four

Confidentiality

Importance

As a buyer, at some point or part of your investigation, you will want to interview employees, customers and suppliers. Sellers are not likely to be comfortable with you doing so, and for good reason. Inept interviews or premature disclosure of the fact that the owner is looking to sell can kill a business. This hurts the seller, and it hurts a potential buyer as well if they plan on the business staying alive after the transaction closes.

First of all, and most importantly, employees may begin to jump ship if they hear a sale is in the offing. In today's world of constant, periodic downsizing and streamlining, most employees get a little worried about job security at even the slightest hint of management change. But when the whispers of a sale spread, there is an octave shift in the employee's inner thinking. Those who are content start thinking about other options, other life goals and career directions. Those who are not content but were held down by the gravity of a constant paycheck begin dusting off their resume. With a potential sale and future change, a paycheck is no longer guaranteed. And, no longer weighted down, many employees consider their self-imposed waiting period over, and soon begin searching.

The ripple effect of a businesses' good and even discontented employees looking for new work can range from troubling to devastating. Troubling from the sense that most industry or business groups are small, at least on a regional basis, and word will travel fast that your business is up for sale.

Soon your competitors will be using that bit of gossip, true or not, against you. Devastating in the sense that if your employee talent pool leaves, if you suffer a major brain drain, a buyer won't want to buy your business anyway. Confidentiality can make or break a deal.

Secondly, customers of many small businesses are generally as loyal to the owner of the business as they are to the company's products or services. If their business dealings have been conducted with mutual respect and integrity, the owner can mean more than, or even embody, the product or service. A new owner thrown into the mix can change that chemistry. And again, the whisper of a sale can shift the customer's octave. A contented customer may start thinking about trying out new suppliers. It is best for both buyer and seller that those thoughts never arise. By keeping everything confidential until the appropriate time, and then explaining, comforting and easing the customer into the new relationship, the seller can sell something worth selling – a business with customers. And a buyer can buy something worth buying – a business with customers.

Suppliers also build relationships with business owners. Specifics of deals are often tailored to the needs of particular customers. Favorable terms are often granted on the basis of stability and track record. A sale may mean instability. A new owner may mean no measurable track record. The whisper of a sale may mean that many years of dealings, even if the sale doesn't go through, are back to square one. Keep your sales prospects confidential for as long as you can.

To cover these risks, a savvy seller will retain legal counsel to draft clauses in contracts and agreements guarding against and/or giving guidelines for disclosure. If a buyer violates these clauses, he or she could be held legally liable. For these reasons, buyers will likely want an attorney's help for this phase of discovery, no matter how willing or open the seller and others may seem. Some buyers and sellers jointly conduct the interviews as a means of protecting against improper or unwanted disclosures.

Ideally, neither buyer nor seller will be making any announcements regarding the deal until after it is done. In this way, each can address concrete worries rather than dealing with the nebulous worry of the unknown.

Prevent Fishing Expeditions

Buying or selling a business is a long, complicated process. The last thing a buyer wants is a seller who isn't sure if he or she really wants to sell. The last thing a seller wants is a buyer who doesn't know what he or she wants to buy. Either scenario can cause a waste of time and money. For a deal to make its way smoothly through the process, there needs to be a motivated buyer and a motivated seller. These are folks who are serious about the process, seasoned enough to have realistic expectations and enlightened enough to know what they want. You don't want a buyer or seller just out fishing for deals, or worse, trolling for free information about your business. If you find one of these, cut your line of contact and move on.

Our next case is illustrative.

Case No. 5 – Marie and Veronica

Marie had a successful bakery business in a large urban area. She had started out with one small bakery in a distant suburb. Word spread of her outstanding confections, and especially her prize-winning berry flavored cheesecakes, and soon people were driving an hour or more to visit the bakery. To meet the demand, Marie opened another four stores throughout the area. As well, due to the spectacular demand for her light and yet flavorable blueberry, raspberry, cranberry and strawberry cheesecakes, she entered into an arrangement with a large supermarket chain which allowed her product to be distributed throughout a four-state region.

Marie's success did not come without sacrifice. She had to rise every morning at 4:00 a.m. to open the main bakery and get production underway. While her husband had been supportive and did more than his share of the household chores, Marie felt that she was missing seeing her children, now 8 and 11, grow up. It was time for her to consider selling her business, or at least cutting back on her workload by bringing in a partner.

Marie had met a business broker, Kevin, at a Chamber of Commerce mixer. While he was somewhat young, he was personable, enthusiastic and seemed to know his business. Marie discussed her situation with Kevin, who assured her that potential buyers or partners could be reviewed in a confidential manner. He said that there was no need for an attorney at this stage of the game. Once a letter of intent was signed, Kevin said, each side's attorneys would become intimately involved. Better to save the money now on legal fees until the parties were closer to being serious.

Marie agreed with Kevin's strategy and allowed him to confidentially bring her potentially interested parties. The first was a bakery chef from Connecticut named Veronica. She had recently moved to the area and was looking to acquire a bakery business. In their first meeting, Marie and Kevin had questioned Veronica as to whether she had the financial wherewithal to complete a purchase. Veronica insisted that she was backed by an investment banker from Wall Street. When pressed as to who this was, Veronica insisted that the information was confidential and couldn't be disclosed. Marie and Kevin felt that Veronica was sure enough of her financing and allowed the preliminary discussions to move forward.

Veronica indicated that the most important thing for her as a bakery chef was the ingredients and their freshness. She didn't need to see exact recipes but she wanted to see how the various confections were made, and how the facility was laid out for efficiency. This request seemed reasonable to Marie and Kevin. So, the next meeting was set up so that Veronica could closely witness operations and layout of the main bakery.

Veronica arrived at the scheduled time with a notepad, pen and handheld Dictaphone. As the tour began she was consumed with how it was all done. While she talked shop with Marie in a light, conversational manner, her questions indicated a keen interest in how the lightness and fresh flavor of the berry cheesecakes was achieved. Veronica stated her investment banker indicated that if she couldn't match Marie's freshness, there would be no deal. With that, Marie, who was liking the idea of spending quality time with her children more and more, was forthcoming with sensitive information.

Veronica completed her fact-finding tour. And she never came back. Kevin was mystified by this. He couldn't explain Veronica's disappearance.

Marie was suspicious. Veronica had not come into the business for no reason at all.

Within a month they had their answer. They couldn't prove it, but Marie knew what had happened.

A rival supermarket chain began distributing light, flavorful berry cheesecakes under the name of Margo's Cheesecakes. They were priced a dollar under Marie's offerings, and they were an immediate hit. The chain that carried Marie's cheesecakes was concerned. At a dollar less, Margo's Cheesecakes were outselling Marie's. The chain demanded a price reduction to compete. Marie had no choice but to accept, which put a severe crimp on the business's margin and profitability. Her new business broker estimated that the new pricing structure had devalued her business by several million dollars.

The lesson here is to be very careful about giving out information. It is advisable to protect yourself in writing.

Preparing (And Dissecting) A Confidentiality Agreement

The first step in preventing the unauthorized use, distribution or access to your business records is by creating a Confidentiality Agreement. By requiring a prospective purchaser to first sign a Confidentiality Agreement, you are sending a subtle but powerful message that you are aware of your rights and are prepared to protect them.

What follows is a sample agreement, written from the perspective of, and for the benefit of, a seller. It is not for everyone in every situation, but rather offers a means of explaining important issues to be concerned with in drafting such an agreement. You will want to consult with your attorney before moving ahead in this regard.

CONFIDENTIALITY AGREEMENT

This Agreement is entered into this date by and between [SELLING COMPANY], a [STATE] corporation ("Us," "We," or "Our"), and [PURCHASING COMPANY OR INDIVIDUAL] ("You," or "Your").

WHEREAS, We are engaged in business as [BRIEF DESCRIPTION OF BUSINESS] ("Our Business");

WHEREAS, You are considering acquiring [the assets of or majority ownership in] Our Business;

WHEREAS, You wish to review financial, operational and other information regarding Our Business; and

WHEREAS, We wish to ensure that any information about Our Business provided to You is kept confidential by You.

NOW THEREFORE, IT IS AGREED AS FOLLOWS:

Section 1. Confidential Information. In order to assist You to evaluate a possible acquisition of [the assets of or the issued and outstanding shares of] Our Business, We agree to provide You with materials relating to Our Business, which may include, but are not limited to, financial data, sales and inventory data, customer lists, supplier lists and pricing, trade secrets, techniques, formulae and technical specifications, drawings, models, data, designs, discoveries, software programs, and any other material used by Us in the operation of Our Business. You acknowledge that [some/all] of this information shall be considered confidential information, as shall any other information marked or designated by Us as confidential; whether or not in written form. Such other information shall include material which is known to You as being treated by as confidential by Us; and information about Us and Our Business provided to You by third parties for which the third party is obligated to keep confidential.

Section 2. "You" Defined. You shall be defined as meaning You and/ or any of Your officers, directors, employees, agents, successors, attorneys and assigns.

Section 3. Ownership and Covenant of Non-Competition. You hereby acknowledge that Our Confidential Information is and shall continue to be Our exclusive property, whether or not disclosed or entrusted to You pursuant to this Agreement. You also agree that You shall not take

Our Confidential Information and use it to directly or indirectly compete against Us.

Section 4. Covenant of Nondisclosure; Safeguard of Confidential Information. You agree not to disclose any of Our Confidential Information, directly or indirectly, under any circumstances or by any means, to any third person without Our express written consent. You agree that You will not copy, transmit, reproduce, summarize, quote or make any commercial or other use whatsoever of any of Our Confidential Information without Our express written consent.

Section 5. Irreparable Harm and Remedies. You acknowledge that any disclosure of Our Confidential Information will cause irreparable harm to Us and Our Business. If You fail to abide by this Agreement, We shall be entitled to specific performance, including immediate issuance of a temporary restraining order or preliminary injunction enforcing this Agreement, and to judgment for damages caused by such breach and to any other equitable remedies provided by applicable law, as well as reasonable attorneys fees and costs.

Section 6. Exclusions. This Agreement shall not apply to any information regarding Us now or hereafter voluntarily released by Us to the public, or which otherwise becomes part of the public domain through lawful means.

Section 7. Duration. The obligations set forth in this Agreement shall continue until either We or You notifies the other party that We or You is no longer interested in proceeding with a potential purchase of Our Business. The obligations set forth in this Agreement regarding Confidential Information shall continue beyond the term of this Agreement for the maximum term allowable by a court of equity to maintain and protect all rights in Our Confidential Information.

Section 8. Termination and Return. Either We or You may terminate this Agreement for any reason and in Our or Your complete discretion. Upon termination of this Agreement, or otherwise as requested, You agree to deliver promptly to Us all of Our Confidential Information, in whatever form, that may be in Your possession or control.

Section 9. Assignment. You may not assign or transfer this Agreement without Our prior written consent.

Section 10. Law Governing. You expressly agree that this Agreement shall be governed by and construed in accordance with the laws of the State of [Nevada], *and that any action on this Agreement shall be brought in a court of competent jurisdiction located in* [County, State]. *You agree that this is a mandatory forum selection clause.*

Section 11. Entire Agreement; Modifications Must Be in Writing. This Agreement contains the entire understanding between and among You and Us and supersedes any prior understandings and agreements respecting Our Confidential Information. This Agreement may not be changed orally. All modifications of this Agreement must be in writing and must be signed by each party.

Section 12. Agreement Binding. This Agreement shall be binding upon and continue to the benefit of Our and Your respective officers, directors, heirs, executors, administrators, successors and assigns.

Section 13. Severability. If any provision of this Agreement or the application of such provision shall be held invalid, the remainder of this Agreement shall not be affected thereby and shall remain in full force and effect.

Section 14. Time. Time is of the essence for this Agreement.

IN WITNESS WHEREOF this Agreement has been executed by the parties on the day and year set out below.

Our signature block
[OUR COMPANY NAME]
A [STATE, TYPE] Company

Per: _____
    Authorized Signatory

Date: _____

Your signature block (if You are an individual)

By: _____*signature*_____
   print Your name here , *an Individual*

Date: _____

   OR

Your signature block (if You are a company)
[YOUR COMPANY NAME]
A [STATE, TYPE] Company

Per: _____
    Authorized Signatory

Date: _____

Let's review the terms of this agreement to gain a better understanding. First of all, in contract terms, the "Whereas" clauses serve as a framework. They indicate what the contract is going to be about and why it is being drawn up.

Section 1. Confidential Information

It is important to provide both seller and potential buyer with an idea of what you, as the seller, consider to be confidential information. However, it is also important not to make the definition of confidential information too narrow. Using a general purpose phrase along the lines of *"...information may include, but is not limited to ..."* provides you with the flexibility to fully protect all of your information. The phrase *"... and information about Us and Our Business provided to You by third parties for which the third party is obligated to keep confidential,"* can be used to cover dealings a potential purchaser may have with your third-party suppliers, from a reference check to determining whether the supply of raw materials or other products that supplier currently provides is likely to undergo any changes in the future.

Section 2. "You" Defined

It is important, especially when you are dealing with a potential purchaser that is a corporate entity in its own right, with employees or management, or where the purchaser is being represented or assisted by a business broker or attorney, to make sure that all of these additional people are bound by the terms of the confidentiality agreement.

Section 3. Ownership and Covenant of Non-Competition

This section provides confirmation that a potential purchaser acknowledges that your company's confidential information is its property, and sets the stage for you in the event that a potential purchaser takes your confidential information and uses it to create a competing business. Imagine how Marie could have made use of this clause in particular to protect her cheesecake recipes and processes.

Section 4. Covenant of NonDisclosure;
Safeguard of Confidential Information

In this section, you are reinforcing the idea that a potential purchaser must keep your information confidential and safe from unauthorized parties.

Section 5. Irreparable Harm and Remedies

Here you are confirming that your business will suffer harm from a breach of the confidentiality provisions of this Agreement, and warn a potential purchaser that you will take all legal steps to protect unauthorized use of your company's confidential information, including going to court. And, if you do wind up in court protecting your confidential information from an unscrupulous or careless potential purchaser, you are also putting a potential purchaser on notice that you will seek repayment by them of your legal fees and expenses.

Section 6. Exclusions

This section acknowledges that you may make information public that was previously considered to be confidential under the agreement with no consequences to either yourself or a potential purchaser. You and/or your attorney may not want any exclusions to apply.

Section 7. Duration

This section sets out the length of time a potential purchaser is bound by the confidentiality agreement. It is quite acceptable to have an obligation to maintain confidentiality well beyond the cancellation of negotiations between you and a potential purchaser.

Section 8. Termination and Return

This section allows either party to call off negotiations and terminate the agreement, and requires all material provided to a potential purchaser to be returned upon your request.

Section 9. Assignment

Assignment, in contractual terms, means transferring a party's obligations under an agreement to another party. Here, you don't want other individuals or companies becoming a part of this Agreement without your written permission.

Section 10. Law Governing

It is important to control where any litigation or arbitration takes place as well as which state's laws apply. You want to make sure that any disputes are resolved in your choice of venue, be it state courts or state arbitration boards. As with sports, think in terms of home court advantage.

Section 11. Entire Agreement; Modifications Must Be in Writing

This clause makes it clear that any verbal agreements or prior agreements you may have had with a potential purchaser are superseded by this written agreement, and that if there are to be any modifications of the terms, the modifications must be in writing, and signed by both you and the potential purchaser.

Section 12. Agreement Binding

In many cases you want to make it clear that the agreement continues beyond you and the potential purchaser personally. For example, if a potential purchaser were to die while in negotiations to purchase your business, his or her estate could not breach the provisions of the agreement.

Section 13. Severability

This section allows for unenforceable sections to be dropped without negating the entire agreement. For example, there may be situations in which courts in different jurisdictions will view a confidentiality agreement as too restrictive. You don't want one clause to be interpreted as unenforceable by a court thus causing the entire agreement to fail. The severability clause prevents that result.

Section 14. Time

Here you are obligating the parties to act in a timely manner. You don't want someone dragging their feet one way or another.

So, that's a confidentiality agreement from a seller's point of view. Now, what does that same agreement look like from a purchaser's point of view?

With any luck it has been drafted fairly and reasonably, and, as long as you are a good-faith potential purchaser, should not pose an onerous obligation on you. Confidentiality agreements are designed to protect a seller's business, not to prohibit you from considering purchasing various businesses, even if those businesses are similar, or identical. If an agreement restricts you from looking at other businesses while in discussions with a potential seller, or restricts you from purchasing a competing business for any length of time, be wary. Also be wary as a buyer if the agreement covers confidential information that really isn't all that confidential or special. You don't want a jilted seller complaining that you are competing against him and using his trade secrets when those secrets are really just common business practices.

Signatures

A confidentiality agreement does not mean an end to concerns about the other side's intentions. Many buyers will sign one just to get to the next level with you, and then waste your time at the next level.

Sellers, to avoid fishing expeditions, consider the following:

- Has the buyer at least begun the process of comparing personal skills, analyzing independent financing capabilities and establishing personal goals?

- Has the buyer researched his or her financing capabilities with bankers, accountants and lawyers?

- How long has the buyer been looking and what has he or she found?

- Does the buyer seem to understand what it takes to run a business?

- Is he or she flexible?

- Is he or she decisive?

Buyers should consider the following:

- Does the seller have historical data based on fact or only pro-forma information about what might occur in the future?

- Does the seller have three to five years of past tax records for your review?

- Is the seller asking for a down payment disproportionate to the asking price (more than one year's worth of reconstructed profit)?

- Does the seller have realistic expectations of the sale?

- Is he or she flexible?

- Is he or she decisive?

If either the buyer or seller has concerns about the other, caution is appropriate. As in Marie's case, a fishing expedition can be devastating for a seller. For a buyer, a seller that is trying to sell blue sky and a glorious future without any sort of backup documentation may be a risk worth avoiding.

When marketing your business opportunity it is important to know that not every inquiry will - or should - lead to a sale. Furthermore, confidentiality, discretion and judgment are considerably more valuable to you than a good set of marketing materials. You are buying or selling a business, not a tube of toothpaste. There is a difference.

However, that distinction can be blurred in the case of franchise operations, which are essentially in the business of selling businesses.

Rich Dad's Tips

- Confidentiality in the sale of a business for a seller is like being in a witness protection program. If the protection of secrets is too weak, or ends unexpectedly, the results can get ugly.

- Sellers should keep their guard up at all times, even if a confidentiality agreement has been signed.

- When it comes to fishing expeditions be a shark not a tuna. Don't get caught in a net of extraction.

When it comes to selling a business there is no greater phenomena than ...

Chapter Five

Franchises

The Franchise Phenomena

They are incredible statistics. Nearly 40% of all retail sales occur through franchise outlets. Total sales by franchisees exceed one trillion dollars per year. Over 15 million people are employed by franchise businesses. Franchises are ubiquitous and a mainstay of pop culture. Some cynics of retail entertainment call us the United Franchises of America. Cynic or not, no one can deny that franchises are a permanent part of our landscape.

As a method of doing business, franchising has far expanded from its early incarnations of gas stations and automobile dealerships into almost every good and service imaginable. By accepting a franchisor's right to sell a specific and unique service or product, combined with the training on how to sell it, the franchisee can minimize their risk by following a proven path. Of course, there is a fee for such experience - usually an initial up-front fee followed by a continuing percentage of gross sales, as well as other sundry fees and costs.

A key element in understanding a franchise opportunity is a careful review of the Franchise Disclosure Document (FDD), sometimes called the Uniform Franchise Disclosure Document. Previously these were called the Uniform Franchise Offering Circular or UFOC. As UFOC turned out to be one of the least pleasing acronyms in modern memory the name of the document has been thankfully changed and will be referred to as the FDD. In the FDD you will be made aware of all the fees involved, and they can be substantial.

But many will argue that whatever the fees are, they are worth it. The brand recognition, the uniformity of business operations (based on previous success) and the shared volume buying power a franchisor provides are only a few of the reasons cited by successful franchisees for why they will only buy an established, well-known franchise. Still, even the truest of the true believer franchisees will caution that owning a franchise does not mean freedom from dedication and effort. You are still running a business. You've got to make it work.

Similarly, when acquiring a franchise, you are still buying a business. You still need to ask the right questions, take the prudent precautions and make the right decisions.

Our next case is illustrative.

Case No. 6 – Vivian and Tomas

Vivian and Tomas had worked very hard for the last six years to save up enough money to pursue a franchise business. It was their dream to own their own business, and they felt that owning a proven retail franchise would give them a leg up on success.

Vivian had begun analyzing franchise opportunities over two years ago. Tomas was working two and a half jobs to achieve their dream and didn't have time for the search. Vivian was pleased to do it for it meant so much to her to do it right.

While both she and Tomas worked in the food service industry, she wasn't sure if a restaurant was right for them or not. So she cast as wide a net as possible by reviewing a multitude of magazine ads and websites for franchise information. She took Tomas to franchise expo shows when they came to town. And in reviewing the myriad of opportunities, Vivian developed her own checklist of information that was important to her, which included:

- What is the franchisor's reputation in the industry and among its franchisees?

- Is the product or service unique?

- Will the product or service be outmoded or passé in five or ten years?

- Will there be competition in the marketplace?

- Will there be competition in the future?

- How many franchisees are there? Have any of them sued the franchisor?

- What is the quality of the franchisor's marketing, advertising and public relations programs?

- How much does each program cost each franchise?

- Will the franchisor's name and reputation make a difference with their customers?

- Is franchise location important? Can it be operated from home? If not, how much will improvements cost?

- After all the expenses and franchise fees are paid, what is the break-even point? Beyond that, can enough of a profit be made to make it all worthwhile?

The last question for Vivian was the most important one to answer properly. Would it all be worthwhile? Would the extra up-front fee and then continuing franchise royalty on their grosses result in more business and greater revenues from franchising than from opening a non-franchise business themselves?

Vivian didn't know the answer to that one. Certainly the franchisees she met at the expos and the ones she called for references on various franchise opportunities seemed to be pleased with their arrangements. But she acknowledged, you weren't likely to meet disgruntled former franchisees at a happy, upbeat opportunity expo and franchisors rarely gave out the names of sour grapes operators for referral purposes. She acknowledged there was an element of faith at work in making the right decision. But their faith had to be divine, for she knew she would most likely only get one chance to get it right.

Eventually Vivian came across a franchise opportunity that fit both her criteria and interest. Salvador's was a unique taqueria restaurant business that was expanding rapidly throughout the southwestern United States. Salvador's served the authentic and pleasing food of El Salvador, open-faced tacos, carne quisada, chicken rellenos, stuffed bananas and other popular items from the Central American country. Both Vivian and Tomas could envision El Salvadoran food becoming a popular mainstream offshoot of Mexican cuisine in the same way that Thai food is to Chinese cuisine.

After discussing the opportunity among friends and family and reviewing the FDD — the federally required disclosure document, they decided to proceed. They put up a $5,000 deposit and began looking for an 800 square foot downtown location for their taqueria business.

Then they learned of a very big problem. A friend of a friend had also acquired a Salvador's franchise. He was also looking to put one in a downtown location. Tomas was furious. He called the Salvador's franchise representative and demanded an explanation.

The representative calmly told him to carefully read the FDD. Salvador's didn't guarantee a specific territory. They could sell to anyone, anywhere. And if one franchisee wanted to open up across the street from another, so be it. It wasn't likely to happen, the representative indicated, since it wasn't in either party's best interests, but under the agreement he signed, it could happen just the same.

Tomas was livid. He was not paying for a non-exclusive territory. El Salvadoran food was hardly that popular and starting out the last thing he needed was two of the same restaurants competing for the same downtown dollar.

The representative politely told Tomas that his franchise did not offer any sort of territorial exclusivity and that he would have to live with downtown competition. With that, Tomas became unglued. He claimed misrepresentation and fraud and demanded his $5,000 deposit back. Even more politely, the representative indicated that the deposit was non-refundable. He could decide not to pursue the Saslvador's franchise, but he would never see the $5,000 again. It said so right in the FDD.

The lesson here is that the FDD must be carefully read and clearly understood. It is strongly suggested that you have it reviewed by your team of advisors, especially your attorney and accountant. Their counsel and opinion on the suitability of the franchise, its management, history and operational strengths and weaknesses should be sought out and considered.

You may also want to contact the International Franchise Association (IFA) in Washington, DC for useful franchise-related articles and information on franchising. Members of the IFA have pledged to adhere to certain business ethics. It may be helpful to know whether a potential franchisor has agreed to such ethical standards.

As well, you will not want to sign up with a franchisor that cannot provide a FDD. It is a federally-mandated document designed to disclose all material information to a prospective franchisee. By law it must be provided by the franchisor at least ten days prior to a franchisee signing a franchise agreement. If a salesman can't give you a copy of one, move on.

There are twenty-three key information categories disclosed in a FDD. It is useful to consider the importance of each one.

1. The Franchisor. General background and historical information is provided here along with relevant discussions of business operations, competition and the nature of the franchise being sold. This is the Executive Summary of the FDD.

2. Management. Each responsible individual within the franchisor and their business experience are detailed. Consider each individual's background. You won't want to buy an auto parts franchise when management's only experience is in selling portable spas. Of course, you may want to stay away from any franchise in which management's experience is in the spa business.

3. Litigation. Read this section first. It will give you a great deal of insight into the franchisor and how it operates. Does it work together with its franchisees? Or, as this section will reveal, is it out to squeeze and seek advantage wherever it can.

4. Bankruptcy. Here, the franchisor, its predecessors, officers and directors must disclose whether they have gone bankrupt or reorganized under the bankruptcy laws during the last fifteen years. Be careful if the officers have bankrupted a number of spa businesses over the years.

5. Franchise Fees. The fees due upon signing the agreement and the method of payments are disclosed here. This is the section Tomas should have read more carefully for it also discloses whether the fees are refundable or not.

6. Other Fees. If you really want to know what you're in for – or don't want to be a part of – read this section first. The fees that you may encounter will range from fair to incredible. These include the standards such as royalty payments, advertising contributions and training fees. From there they can veer into audit fees, lease negotiation fees, transfer fees, renewal fees and consulting fees. In this section, fee does not rhyme with free.

    Be sure to understand how any royalties are calculated. If they are based on a percentage of sales, then how are sales calculated? And how do such royalties compare with other franchise operators?

7. Franchisee's Initial Investment. This section discloses, usually in a chart format, the estimated costs the franchisee will pay to get the business open. This will include equipment, fixtures, tenant improvement, working capital and similar costs. This is a section for your accountant to perform a reality check on.

8. Purchase Requirements. If the franchisee is obligated to purchase supplies, inventory and the like from designated sources it is disclosed herein. So is what the franchisor is making off such required source purchases.

9. Approved Supplier Specifications. Equipment specifications, supplier programs and the like are disclosed in this section along with, again, whether the franchisor is financially benefitting from such requirements.

10. Financing. The terms and conditions of any financing the franchisor may offer franchisees is detailed. Be careful to consider any default or acceleration clauses that may be involved, which must be disclosed in this section.

11. Franchisor Obligations. This telling section identifies the initial and ongoing services and support the franchisor offers. Here will be detailed the training, advertising, inventory control and other services offered by the franchisor company. Satisfy yourself that the franchisor has an interest in supporting your continued success.

12. Exclusive Territory. An important element of any franchise arrangement. Just what are you getting? Exclusive or non-exclusive? Do you have the option or right of first refusal to expand the territory? Can you lose your territory if certain sales quotas aren't met? Can the company compete against you by establishing its own company-owned stores in the territory once you've paved the way? Read this one carefully. Make sure the boundaries of any territory are specifically defined, county by county, city by city, street by street.

13. Trademarks, Trade Names, Etc. The status of any federal and/or state protection of trademarks, trade names and other intellectual property must be disclosed. If the franchisor does not have a registered trademark think twice about continuing. As well, if there are infringement cases or other litigation involving the franchise's intellectual property, be sure to have your attorney review them. One of the most valuable assets a franchise has is its trademark. If it is to be lost in litigation, then what do you have? Not much.

14. Patents and Copyrights. The same issues apply as in Section 13.

15. Franchise Management. Whether or not the franchisor allows absentee ownership or other management arrangements is detailed here.

16. Offer Restrictions. If any goods and services may not be offered by a franchisee that information must be disclosed.

17. Franchise Termination, Renewal and Transfer. If things don't work out and/or the franchisor jerks the franchise, what are the procedures to be followed? If the franchisee must sell, how is it handled? Those issues are dealt with in this section, an important one to review and consider.

18. Celebrity Endorsements. How much do those famous fellows get for hawking tacos? And what percent do they own of the company? You'll learn this in Item 18.

19. Earning Claims. If the franchisor is willing to project earnings for a prospective franchisee that information is included in this section. If they are not willing to do so (and believe me, I wouldn't let my client do it - unless, that is, they really liked getting sued) a statement indicating that no earnings claims are offered is instead inserted.

20. Franchisee Information. The number of franchisees and where they are located is included, usually in a chart format. As well, any terminated or non-renewed franchises in the last three years are noted. This section helps one understand geographic scope and success of the franchise and also alerts one as to the problem areas for the company.

21. Financial Statements. A complete financial statement is included here for your CPA to review with great care. He or she should not allow you to buy passage aboard a sinking ship. Pay attention to how much debt the company has. Are your franchise monies going into brand enhancement and advertising? Or to pay off the loans used to settle the last three lawsuits. Also, can you verify what is being presented? You may want to check with Dun & Bradstreet or another credit agency for confirming information, as well as to learn if the bills are being paid on time.

22. Franchise Agreement. The franchise agreement itself, along with any other documents to be signed by both parties, is included here.

23. Acknowledgment of Receipt. The last page is used to acknowledge receipt by the franchisee of the FDD.

As you review the FDD the problem areas, if any, will be identified. You will consider a number of issues, including:

- Can the franchisor terminate the franchise for almost any breach at all?

- Are there highly restrictive covenants not to compete upon termination?

- Are the renewal fees and terms so excessive as to make one suspicious that the franchisor wants your efforts to lead to a company-owned store?

- Do a multitude of nickel and dime fees add up to a pound of flesh?

- Is the intellectual property and entire identity of the franchisor in danger of being lost?

- Does the franchisor provide any pre-opening and grand opening support? Why not?

- Who pays for all these marketing materials?

- Do you get the sense that the franchisor really likes litigation?

- Does the franchisor assert a little too much control over areas it has absolutely no business at all being involved in?

- Are there any standards whatsoever for how advertising and marketing dollars are allocated and spent in your local market?

- Is there an active franchise association and a procedure for dealing with grievances? How many grievances have there been lately?

- Do franchisees have any say at all in operational decisions or policies?

As the tone of the previous questions indicates, you need to proceed into this arena with a healthy dose of skepticism. Yes, there are a number of very ethical and successful franchise companies in the marketplace. There is no denying that fact. But also remember that the FDD is not passed over by any governmental agency. While the information is required to be disclosed there is no one out there reviewing the information to determine if it is accurate. Except you.

Do your due diligence with the assistance of your advisor team and you'll make the right decision.

Rich Dad's Tips

- Carefully analyze whether the benefits and drawbacks of franchising are for you.

- Know every fee associated with your desired franchise to avoid later surprises.

- FDD's are intentionally boring documents that may literally lull you to sleep. Be sure to read over them several times when you are fresh and clear headed in order to obtain a full understanding of what you are getting into.

- Feel free to download our complimentary report "Winning With Franchises" found at www.corporatedirect.com.

Now let's review the information that non-franchise sellers should provide ...

Chapter Six

Selling Prospectus

Importance

A selling prospectus (also known as a marketing brochure or offering memorandum), at its simplest, is a company profile designed to market a business to prospective buyers. Its goal is to generate interest and justify the asking price. It can be used in select and limited targeted market mailings, to supplement interviews and to support brief personal phone inquiries. This is not a mass-mailing tool. After you have established a relationship with a prospective buyer (and have a signed non-disclosure agreement), you may want to use a more detailed prospectus. You will want an attorney to look over your prospectus with you to make sure it doesn't contain anything that will haunt you later.

For sellers, the selling prospectus is not only a useful marketing tool, but a valuable learning tool as well. While setting out key information used for preliminary screening by buyers, it also forces the seller to get clear in his or her own head exactly what he or she wants from the sale – both financially and personally. Preparation of a prospectus organizes the seller's thoughts for eventual personal discussions with prospective buyers. If so authored, the prospectus may also offer the added benefit of seller anonymity. By keeping the business name and address confidential you can have interested parties contact a separate phone line instead of showing up at your door and gossiping throughout the industry about a sale.

The nature of selling a business is unlike that of most any other sale. With business transfers, it is the seller who is most active. He or she is trying hard to convince buyers that the deal is a good one, that the company has growth potential and that the historical data prove it. A seller cannot just sit behind the counter and wait for the buyer to discover the deal. He or she must actively pursue buyers, and then actively prove the business' worth. The selling prospectus is the most valuable tool the seller has in this arena, so it has to be good.

The selling prospectus should be more than a dull documentation of facts. It should be a persuasive advertisement as well. In fact, you may want to bring in a public relations or copywriting expert to help draft it. At a minimum, be sure it is written well – no typos, no grammar errors, no misspelled words. It should be brief, clear and straightforward. If your prospectus seems unprofessional, so will you and the business you are trying to sell.

If properly prepared, the prospectus can help buyers eliminate companies from the running. A buyer should be able to tell if the business suits his or her needs, is financially within reach and whether or not it meets his or her skill level. It should spark interest, but not satisfy. Buyers will either reject businesses through the prospectus or form more specific questions. Either way, it benefits the seller. Weeding out bad matches decreases confidentiality concerns. Whetting a true buyer's appetite increases interest.

Elements

There is no consistent format for a selling prospectus. It is not a legal document, with specific legal requirements, in the way that a FDD or a private placement memorandum (PPM) is a legal document. As you may know, a PPM, which is also commonly and confusingly called a prospectus, is used for the private, non-registered sales of securities (stock) in a business. Like a FDD, a PPM is subject to state and federal requirements regarding the information that must be disclosed. As well, a PPM has restrictions on the manner in which the sales of securities are solicited and offered. A selling prospectus, however, does not have such formal requirements. You are in charge of what information is left in and what is left out. Unlike a FDD or a PPM, it is not a heavily formulaic document, but rather a marketing document that represents your unique and creative effort to sell your unique and individual business.

Nevertheless, as with a FDD or a PPM, you must not make material misstatements of fact in your selling prospectus. If you claim that your product was voted Number One by the readers of a magazine that doesn't exist, you're in for trouble. Even if the magazine does exist, but what you claim was a Number One finish was really only a top ten placement, you are creating future problems for yourself. False claims and exaggerated come ons are not appropriate. A buyer who relies on such statements to their detriment can – and most likely will – sue over the infraction. (We'll review just such a case ahead). They will demand rescission of the contract, all of their money back, and damages for their trouble. You don't want such problems. Granted, the selling prospectus is a marketing document designed to generate interest, but it can and should be drafted so that the truth be told.

Until you have that confidentiality and non-disclosure agreement signed or have at least met with prospective buyers in person, you should leave out information about:

- specific location
- company name or address
- detailed listings of hard assets
- financial statements

The task at hand is to solicit interest, not generate an offer. You want to keep things somewhat secretive, and certainly confidential, until you can get a sense of who is looking. You may want to do your own due diligence on any potential buyers. Knowing whether they can actually financially do the deal or not can save a lot of wasted effort. There are plenty of looky-loos out there who are quite willing to waste your time and money (as well as, oddly enough, their own) in order to feel important. As we saw in Marie's case, there are also plenty of hard-nosed competitors ready to misrepresent themselves in order to steal your trade secrets. So find out who is really inside that Trojan horse before you let them in. And use the selected information in your selling prospectus to get that horse sniffing at you, rather than galloping off to their own paddock with all of your inside information.

The following is a short summary of some of the most common sections in a selling prospectus, along with a discussion of what to include on the high end of disclosure. You may want to omit some of this information if your prospectus will be going out to people with whom you have not met and/or signed a non-disclosure agreement, or consider using the more abbreviated version commencing on page 73.

1. Investment Summary: Though this section usually comes first in the document, it is written last. Everything in the prospectus is designed to support this section. Usually only one or two pages, it should whet the reader's appetite and address the reasons for selling, what is for sale, timeframe of the sale, asking price and financing requirements. Everything in this section should virtually scream: "Buy me!"

2. General Company Presentation: A simple overview of the company is presented here. Include the age of the company; how, why and by whom it was formed; why it has been successful so far; details on location(s), employees and annual sales; what is sold and how; what marketing tools are/have been used; general information on proprietary technology, intellectual property and processes; what the future holds in terms of marketing, products, services or overall business plans (be general), why the company is for sale (in positive terms).

3. Overall Market Assessment: No company operates in a vacuum. Here you explain the relationship between the overall market, the specific industry and the company for sale. A three to five year historical analysis of growth trends should be included along with a discussion of future market trends.

4. Sales and Marketing Overview: This section offers the opportunity to brag a little and show that the company's success is no accident. Discuss the strategic focus of the company, details of products and services, marketing strategies, personnel makeup, distribution, historical successes, future goals and what makes the company approach unique. You may want to include some competitive information for comparison for a buyer not familiar with the industry. Any special customer agreements or arrangements would fall under this section along with general background of key marketing and sales personnel. A detailed analysis of products, successes (and non-injurious struggles) and customers may be appropriate as well.

5. Special Assets, Process and Agreements: Just as the heading implies, this is where you lay out general information about proprietary information, such as patents, trademarks and copyrights held by the company. (A copyright is a protection of a written expression such as a book, play or advertising. A patent is a protection of a better device, design or process substantially unique enough to be considered novel or non-obvious. A trademark is a registered name of a product or service sold by a particular company.) Special agreements with foreign countries, distributors and vendors, as well as details of intellectual property are included here. You include all this information (as with all information in the prospectus) to show that the asking price is fair. But again, you only provide general information about your intellectual property assets. Specifics can wait until you are much further down the line with a potential buyer.

6. Key Management Personnel: You don't need to name names (though it would help if you have a non-disclosure agreement), but you will want to include information on key personnel here. Detail the educational, professional and pertinent personal backgrounds of the CEO, President, Vice Presidents, Directors, key board members, key technology personnel, key operations personnel, staff consultants, investors and others who are important to company

operations. Include enough information to show these are credible professionals who have chosen to work for your company and advance its prospects.

7. Past Financial Performance: You may or may not want to include financial statements for the past three to five years. Information such as comparative statements for the most current year and the year previous, an overview of accounting procedures, steps used to orient the statements and special situations that caused radical dips or jumps in performance, may assist in attracting a serious buyer, or it may provide too much information to the wrong people. Whether to use financials or not in your initial selling prospectus is a judgment call on your part. Obviously, as things get serious between the buyer and seller this information will have to be provided.

8. Projected Future Financial Performance: This section can also be tricky, so get your attorney on board. You don't want to be making any potential misrepresentations here. Be sure that your future forecasts are worded as estimates (guesses), not commitments (guarantees). The difference between a guess and a guarantee is that there is no guessing about whether or not you'll be sued on a guarantee. You will. Nevertheless, you shouldn't automatically skip this section out of fear of the legalities. If you present the information properly, with enough conditional "no-guarantee" language, an argument can be made that future financials is one of the best justifications for your asking price.

9. Ownership Structure: Often dull for everyone but the listed owners, but usually necessary, this is the section about who owns what and for how long. Be sure to check and see if everyone in the selling group wants their name initially listed. More people want privacy than you would expect. And not everyone wants their name circulating as the owner of a lucrative business for sale.

10. Asking Price and Financing: You arrived at a price logically, right? Here's where you spell out that logic. Any special financing provided or required should be included in this section.

11. Conclusion: If they didn't get it in the summary, here's your chance to reiterate your selling points. Remind the reader of the excellent investment opportunity offered and, using the old real-estate broker's gambit, urge rapid movement forward before someone else comes along to snap up the deal.

12. Appendices: Web site information, brochures, samples, competitive details, biographies and anything else that might support the contents of the prospectus can be added as appendices and referenced in the body of the report.

In case you want to use a more general and less-detailed prospectus to get buyers interested in personal meetings, you may want to use the following outline:

1. Company history and background: include company formation, mission, marketing segments and future business activity

2. Location: include general area only

3. Assets: generalized description of value, age, condition, leases or owned facilities without listing specifics

4. Operations: business hours, dips and jumps in production, advertising and PR activity, marketing efforts, production events and any unique aspects of the business

5. Employees: broad general workforce information, payment plans and employee benefits

6. Confidentiality Statement: brief reminder that customers, employees and suppliers are not aware of a pending sale

7. Sales: general and vague information about sales and principal buyers that does not give advantage to competitors who might read the document

8. Competition: where the business ranks and how it could be improved

9. Skill Level: describe your own skills and you will have a pretty good description of what is needed for a potential buyer

10. Selling Terms: form of present ownership, tax issues, how and why you arrived at the specific price, asking price and conditions of financing, reasons for selling

11. Financials: description of record-keeping maintenance, highlights of sales, operating expenses and reconstructed cash flow

12. Interviews: explanation as to how to set up a personal interview

However you decide to use your prospectus, whether as a preliminary marketing tool or an invitation for further investigation, you should draft the report yourself. No one knows your business better than you. You can bring in experts for advice and literary clean-up, but do the first draft yourself.

Preliminary Questions for Buyers

As you might surmise, in my practice I have assisted many buyers in analyzing business acquisitions and preparing business plans. Over the years I have developed a checklist of ten preliminary questions a buyer should ask when considering a business purchase. The Top Ten are:

- Is the business in a growth industry?
- Is the business gaining market share?
- What am I buying? Cash flow, assets, customers?
- What is the return on investment? How does that compare to industry averages?
- What advantages does the business have over competitors?
- What are the revenue streams and margins?
- How many customers?
- How many customers make up 80% of sales?
- What is the customer retention rate? Current and anticipated under new ownership?
- What is the exit strategy?

Analyzing Operations

Once the preliminary questions are answered to the buyer's satisfaction, greater information should be sought out. The prospectus may or may not provide that information. Some additional issues that buyers should be interested in are:

- Sales: products, lines, marketing, profit centers, competition, seasonality

- Leases: transferability, length of time, whether or not a change in the purpose clause is permitted

- Loan agreements: amount, security, status, transferability of assets, transferability of stock

- Contracts: amounts, status, transferability

- Supplier relations: number, size, status of credit, satisfaction

- Customer relations: number, size, frequency, satisfaction, active or inactive, geography

- Personnel: number, titles, duties, value of each, salaries, satisfaction, promised benefits, special rights, privileged duties, fringe benefits, policy manual, whether or not there are any collective bargaining agreements

- Proprietary information (copyrights, trademarks, patents): types, protection, status, ownership, expiration

- Plant and equipment: ownership, age, value, make and model, serial numbers, life span, capacity, compliance with federal health and safety standards, transferability

If some of the information listed above is not in the selling prospectus and you, as buyer, want more information, the seller has done their job.

Rich Dad's Tips

- A seller's prospectus that keeps the wrong type of buyers away has done its job as well as one that attracts acceptable buyers.

- While puffery is normal, never deviate away from the truth when drafting a prospectus. The consequences may be less than enjoyable.

- As a buyer be sure to have answered any questions not satisfactorily addressed in the prospectus.

The buyer's next step is to contact the seller for more. And probably the most important information sought will be ...

Chapter Seven

Financials

The primary way a buyer judges a target business is by the numbers. Financial reports must be accurate, credible and meet professional standards.

The fact that you, as the seller, have had a CPA assist you with your financials, and perhaps can have that CPA available to explain his work, can be a huge advantage in the process.

The way a seller runs a business before and during the sale must be geared toward increasing the likelihood of completing the sale. The best way to increase that likelihood is by keeping an eye on the numbers. A sale doesn't happen overnight. Financial decisions must be made. Just make sure you keep the financial reports in mind when you make such decisions. Do you need to spend more money than necessary for a new piece of equipment? Will that purchase help your financials, and your ability to sell the business? The state of your financials can dictate the ease and speed of a sale, the price you get and even whether or not a sale even goes through.

Buyers use financial facts from the past to determine financial hopes of the future. Cast your historical reports with accurate, but positive views so that positive pro-forma projections will make sense. If recent changes cause large deviations for the future, explain them in your reports. Again, as the seller, you and your accountant need to be able to explain the financials. You may want to hold practice sessions where one of you plays the buyer and asks the hard questions about the financials. Such an exercise can sharpen up your explanations.

The place to start with financials is with the current state of affairs. You need to understand not only what the numbers mean, but how they were arrived at as well. Whether you realize it or not, you have accounting procedures. They can range from documented, regimented updates to receipts in a shoebox, but they are procedures nonetheless. If your procedures are tacit rather than deliberate, you need to realize such lack of planning will show in your financials. One of the things a potential buyer will want to see is an accounting of your procedures and policies. How the numbers are prepared will reflect on your overall business acumen and professionalism. Think about how you want your company to be perceived. You want the buyer to purchase and pay for a full-fledged going concern, not a project that needs to be fixed.

Buyers should have their own accountants on board. Don't take any numbers at face value without at least reading all the fine print on the financial reports. Verify methods of accounting, especially concerning recognition of revenues or expenses. And be sure to find out if the accountant prepared statements with his or her own numbers or those given to him or her by the seller. The seller's accountant who prepares financials with just the numbers provided by the seller may be just as in the dark as anyone else.

What if the seller is not forthcoming with the financial reports? He or she very well may not. A buyer may offer to sign a confidentiality agreement up front in order to allay some of the seller's fears of disclosing protected financial information. Or the buyer may have his or her accountant make the request and look at the reports. The fact that a buyer is willing to pay an accountant for this helps show his or her seriousness about purchasing the business. But, if a seller will not disclose financial information or if his or her financial information consists of a shoebox full of receipts, move on.

Even so, as recent accounting scandals indicate, the seller may provide all the financial data sought, in perfect order, all of which has been prepared by one of the world's most recognized accounting firms. And you will still have to verify.

Case No. 7 – Paul, Victoria and Danny

Paul was a super salesman. He was personable, glib and totally believable. He could, as they say, sell ice to the Aleuts. Paul was a vice-president of sales and marketing for a large consumer products company. It had been his dream to own and run his own business some day, and with time marching onwards, he was getting anxious to realize his goals. As well, he had become keenly dissatisfied with the corporate bureaucracy he faced at work. He was confident of his skills and knew that if his marketing strategies were fully budgeted and implemented he could dramatically increase sales of his division's product. But instead, the company's president allocated resources away from Paul's division. Paul quietly suspected that it was all political, that the president feared for his job if he allowed Paul to do too well.

Paul had begun looking to buy the right business to satisfy his requirements. It had to be a consumer products company with a good upside for sales. It had to be a company where the missing ingredient was his sales and marketing talent. After consulting with various business brokers, reviewing the classified ads in major national and regional publications, and scouring the Internet's myriad of business opportunities for sale, he found a company that he felt was right in his strike zone.

Victoria, his wife, was worried. She was aware of, and even supportive of, Paul's career objectives. She knew he could sell anything and that he wanted to head up his own company. But she was also cautious and prudent. They had a family and a mortgage and those obligations had to be met. Paul could not just simply buy any business. It had to be the exact right business, not only for Paul, but for his family. There were no second chances for Victoria.

The available company that Paul had located was in the gas barbeque business. They sold their GrillKing models through Wal-Mart, Costco and Sears, as well as other large national retailers. The GrillKing business was a division of a large, publicly-traded conglomerate that was forever shedding its skin (and miscellaneous divisions) and recasting itself as whatever kind of company Wall Street was favoring that half decade. Their new image was financial services and barbequing didn't have the right sizzle to fit in with their most recent recasting.

The purchase price was higher than Paul wanted to pay, but the company had a known brand name in the market, which had value. Paul felt he could build upon that awareness and take the company to the next level of sales. With the help of some friends and family members who, over the years had said they would invest in whatever company Paul wanted to get into, Paul felt he could pull off the deal.

Victoria was now even more nervous. Using their own money was one thing. But taking the money from friends and family was quite another. If it wasn't a success, she couldn't live with herself. She worried that she would be shunned and isolated and have to move if things didn't work out. She needed help and she knew Paul needed help to know if this was the exact right business or not. So she called on the biggest nerd that she knew.

Danny was Victoria's brother. He was a stooped and somewhat disheveled CPA in a small southeastern Missouri town. Danny had a decent practice serving individuals and businesses in his community, but his passion was forensic accounting. This allowed him to play the detective and determine what was really going on behind the numbers. Several times a year he would be retained by a bankruptcy trustee or a court-appointed receiver to figure out from an accounting standpoint what had happened within a failed or disputed company scenario. With his disheveled manner he came across as Colombo with a calculator, and like the TV detective, he always got to the bottom of things.

Victoria needed her brother's help now. Paul was lining up investors and, in the process of convincing them that this was a good deal, he was convincing himself. Victoria got the GrillKing financials to Danny as soon as she could.

It took a few days but Danny eventually called to speak with Victoria and Paul. He had noticed some things in the financials that he wanted to run by them. Paul was not keen to talk to Danny about things, but Victoria insisted.

As the conference call commenced, Danny said the main thing he had noticed was that GrillKing's accounts receivable were growing faster than its sales. Paul was gruffly unconcerned, but Victoria wondered why that was so important. Danny said it raised a concern about the quality of sales. With accounts receivable (money owed to GrillKing for barbeques sold) growing at a greater percentage than sales itself, it could mean that GrillKing was "channel stuffing" to increase short-term results.

Victoria didn't understand. Danny had her look at page four of the financials. In the last three months sales had grown twenty percent over the previous three month period, a significant jump in sales. It made the company look good. But while they had booked a big increase in sales, GrillKing hadn't collected all of the money yet. Accounts receivable, the amount remaining to be paid on those sales, had grown by forty percent in the last quarter. So while the company was selling like there was no tomorrow, they were collecting less.

Paul appeared unconcerned. His company was always offering special terms to generate sales. But Danny countered that the GrillKing promotion was not typical. As a good forensic accountant, he went out in the field. He had gone down to his local Wal-Mart and talked to the manager, who was a client of his. The manager had said he had never seen a promotion the likes of GrillKing's current deal. He said that Wal-Mart could take possession of the grills and not pay for them until they were sold. And if the grills were never sold, they could cancel the order as to those grills and return them.

While Paul said nothing, Victoria asked for further clarification. Danny explained that this was a great deal for Wal-Mart and it made GrillKing look as though it were selling a lot of barbeques. But there was only a short-term benefit to GrillKing. By stuffing the channels of distribution with product, they were sacrificing consistent long-term sales. With numerous grills sitting on the Wal-Mart floor for which no money was owed until they sold, Wal-Mart was not going to be buying any more grills anytime soon. And, if the market shifted away from gas barbeques back to charcoal, or whatever was hot, Wal-Mart could simply return the barbeque without payment, leaving GrillKing stuck with a lot of unsold, and now old, inventory.

As Danny explained it, the near-term outlook for GrillKing in the next few years was not good. And it appeared to him that the parent conglomerate had undertaken a conscious strategy to increase immediate sales in order to justify a higher selling price for the GrillKing division.

That was enough for Victoria. And when it all sunk in, it was enough for Paul. From Danny's point of view, the fact that the conglomerate's CPA auditors allowed the company to book the transactions as completed sales when the barbeques could be returned without payment at any time amounted to a highly improper accounting practice. But then Danny noticed that the national accounting firm had not only been retained to audit the conglomerate's books, but was also receiving millions of dollars in separate, outside consulting fees (a practice which is now outlawed.) As such, the accounting firm was compromised, since they were not an independent, disinterested party. Instead, they were part of the high-dollar gravy train and thus, ethically, off track. The integrity of the conglomerate's entire financial statement was open to question due to this conflict. Danny advised his sister and brother-in-law that it would be hard to trust any of the numbers on the papers given to him.

But Victoria and Paul had already made up their minds. There are many criminals out there and some of them wear expensive suits and frequent the canyons of Wall Street. Danny's independent and clear-eyed review of the financials saved them from being the next victims.

As Robert Kiyosaki's Rich Dad has taught, business and investing are team sports. And especially when you are investing in a business, you need a good accountant on your team. A forensic accountant like Danny, who loves to get behind the numbers and figure out what is really going on, can be extremely useful, especially when you are buying a business with significant revenues and expenses. It is very important to know that just because the financials read as if there is a profit, doesn't mean the business is actually generating one. Bring the right accountant on board to get you closer to the truth.

For both buyers and sellers it is important to know how the financials are presented and what is important within them. A brief review follows.

Balance Sheet

The balance sheet is a snapshot of a company's finances. Usually "taken" at the end of a fiscal period (such as the end of the year), the picture shows the company's net worth and accounting value. Net worth for a company is found through a determination of the value of its assets. The value of these assets is often called a company's "book value." Value is determined by subtracting the amount owed on an object from the amount for which an object can be sold.

However, depreciation allows a company to take an operating expense deduction on an item as its functional life is reduced through use. This depreciation increases as time goes on. Therefore, total asset book value (net worth) is the initial purchase price of all assets minus total depreciation of those assets. You and your accountant may want to look into the true market value of certain assets. A computer with three years of depreciable life on it may be valued at $2,000 for accounting purposes. In reality, that computer may be useless and sitting in the back of someone's closet. That "asset" should be a subject of renegotiation.

The addition of assets increases a company's net worth. Adding liabilities (debt) and taking a depreciation expense deduction decreases a company's net worth.

Shareholder's equity and owner's equity are essentially the same, with the former referring to a group of owners, the latter a single owner. Owner equity may be in the form of retained earnings (net income left over for the year) and paid in capital (money paid by shareholders for stock).

To increase owner equity, assets must increase without an increase in liabilities. If liabilities increase without an increase in assets, owner equity decreases.

The following is a basic outline of a balance sheet:

1. Assets (ranked by liquidity: nearness to cash)
    a. current (cash or able to be turned into cash within 12 months) such as cash, accounts receivable and inventory
    b. long-term (fixed), such as land and equipment

2. Liabilities
   a. current (debts or bills due to be paid within 12 months), such as accounts payable, accruals and interest payable on credit line, as well as prepaid liabilities such as deposits.
   b. long-term (due beyond 12 months), such as long-term notes

3. Owner's Equity (or stockholder's equity or shareholder's equity or net worth or book value), including common stock and retained earnings

What is one of the most important element to understand in this realm? Accounts receivable. How soon will the company get paid?

Ask the seller for an accounts receivable aging analysis. The analysis should ask:

- How many dominant customers are there and how quickly do they pay?

- How many accounts are over 90 days old? (Note that lenders may not accept these as collateral for financing)

- What percentage of debts must be written off?

A large number of accounts more than 90 days outstanding may point to serious problems. Perhaps the seller has become lazy in anticipation of retirement, or maybe the quality of goods sold has gone down and buyers are refusing to pay.

Have your accountant compare actual bad debt history with the amount reserved on the balance sheet to see if the company has allowed enough for bad debts.

Check to see if any receivables are in collection and whether or not they are collectible.

Also see if any receivables are pledged or factored as security for loans. If so, have your accountant review these agreements carefully.

Buyers, beware of large jumps in accounts receivable. As in our previous case, it may be a sign of a seller trying to make the business look better than it really is. In anticipation of the sale, the seller may have extended credit to customers it normally would not.

Some businesses (such as manufacturing) routinely factor receivables in order to guarantee an income stream. This process involves selling receivables to a factor (an intermediary with money) for discounted cash and then notifying debtors that they must now pay the factor rather than the business. If such arrangements exist, buyers need to check them carefully for whether the factor has bought the receivables with or without recourse. With recourse means the business is still liable for the money if the receivable can not be collected upon. Without recourse means the factor loses the money if it can't collect. Either way, the receivables are no longer an asset of the business.

Look for notes receivable. Some will be for the simple cost of doing business, but others may represent money the owner owes the company. In such a case, it is imperative you find out if there is an enforceable promissory note related to the debt. Sometimes when the loan is from the company to the owner of the company, there isn't an enforceable note. You may want to make a provision that any loan amounts be paid at closing or deduct it from the purchase price. Or, you may want to negotiate that the owner's loans are voided as part of the purchase price. Check all notes receivable listed as assets to see that they can be paid within a year. Some notes were once accounts receivable that could not be collected. If they couldn't be collected before, what does that mean for the future? You don't want to pay for illusory promises.

Also check accounts payable. Suppliers will frequently grant the company credit. Be aware of these agreements and the terms involved. Money could be owed the day after you close. Also, be wary if no such agreements exist. It could be simply reflective of the company taking advantage of cash payment discounts or it may be an indication of really awful credit and some nasty surprises.

Notes payable need to be analyzed as well. Check if a security interest in assets has been granted to a lender. Even if the buyer says none of the assets are secured, you will want to do your own "UCC-1" search with the county recorder and the secretary of state for each county and state the company does business in. A feature of the Uniform Commercial Code, a UCC-1 is a publicly recorded financing statement designed to put others on notice that an asset is subject to a loan or security agreement. The agreement may provide that if the asset is transferred, as in the sale of a business, the obligation to pay is accelerated and immediately due. Obviously, as the buyer, you need to know this.

If encumbered by a UCC-1 or other agreement, the assets may not be able to be sold or used as collateral in the future – again, important information. Also check the length of time for repayment. If the note is due within a year, it is a current liability. If it isn't due for more than a year, it should be listed as a long-term debt.

Check for the value of inventory. What appears on the balance sheet is what the company paid for the inventory only. Find out the original cost, fair market value and condition of all inventory items. What cost $10 per unit two years ago may not, due to market changes, obsolescence or just age, be worth anywhere near that amount now. Also break inventory down by raw materials, work in progress and finished goods. Obviously finished goods are worth more than raw materials. You need to know how much of the inventory falls into each category to know what it is all truly worth now.

When looking at cost for inventory, you will want to determine how that cost was arrived at. Prices for materials, labor and finished products change over time. When something was bought is important in determining its cost. Most inventory items aren't labeled individually as to when purchases were made, so figures can reflect either the highs or lows of costs to produce. For purposes of valuing a company, a buyer should go with the conservative estimates and use the higher estimates of production costs. It is better for the buyer to underestimate earnings than to overestimate. Obviously sellers may want to do the opposite.

Fixed assets are generally the big ticket items on the balance sheet. Plant and equipment (fixed) assets may include office furniture, cars and trucks, machinery and other equipment expected to be around for more than a year. These items are depreciated (written off over a period of years) rather than expensed (written off all at once in the year of purchase). While the balance sheet lists these items and lists accumulated depreciation, it does not really tell you about the worth of such items. Depreciation doesn't always have much to do with the useful life of items or have much relation to market value or cost of replacement. The $50,000 truck that is being depreciated over five years may be listed as worth $30,000 after the first two years of use. But if that truck has been rode hard over the last two years in a big construction job, it may not be worth anywhere near its listed value on the company's books. You need to analyze and evaluate the true value of each asset yourself.

There are tax ramifications to fixed assets as well. If the purchase is a stock transfer rather than an asset purchase, the buyer only gets the depreciation that has not already been claimed. This lowers the expenses that can be claimed and raises the tax bill.

As for liabilities, find out to whom the business owes money and what sorts of expenses are incurred. You'll need an accounts payable analysis from the seller for this. The analysis should include:

- terms and amounts due
- specific suppliers
- how many suppliers and any special relationships they have with the seller
- any trade debts in collection
- whether or not loans are current
- rates of interest and terms of loans
- credit rating for the company
- any significant accrued liabilities
- whether or not current tax obligations are current

Remember these liabilities are likely to become yours if you sign a purchase agreement.

The net worth section should give you an idea of how the business was capitalized by its owners. There are usually two components: paid-in-capital (reflecting what the owners contributed) and retained earnings (any earnings retained in the business over the years).

Income Statement

Whereas the balance sheet is a snapshot in time, the income statement (or profit and loss statement or statement of operations) tracks income and expenses in a standardized way, over time (generally a month, quarter or year). The following is an outline:

1. Total Income from Sales (and investments, if applicable). Are sales increasing or decreasing? How are sales divided between products? How many customers are there?
2. Cost of Sales
3. Gross Margin (#1 minus #2)
4. Expenses (salaries, advertising, insurance, rent, repairs, supplies, telephone and utilities)
5. Pre-Tax Profit (#3 minus #4)
6. Taxes
7. Net Income (#5 minus #6)
8. Shareholder Dividends

Shareholder dividends are deducted from net income. Any remaining money is transferred to the balance sheet as retained earnings.

Buyer beware: a high level of returns of goods may mean a large number of shoddy products have been shipped. If this is the case, watch out for lawsuits. Also, as was illustrated in our last case, artificial increases in sales by a seller granting easy credit to customers, some of whom who would normally be turned down, is a possibility. Though these sales show up under sales revenues, they may never bring in any cash.

Buyers should look out for peaks in professional service fees (legal and accounting). A peak in accounting fees could be a sign of an IRS audit. If you see one of these peaks, have an accountant aggressively audit tax returns to try and be sure there is not a large tax bill waiting around the corner. A peak in legal fees could mean a lawsuit was filed. You need to inquire as to whether there is any outstanding litigation or settlement agreements that are an issue. These are crucial matters of which you will certainly want to be aware, and which will affect your buying decision.

You will want to compare gross profit margins to those of others in the industry. Information on industry norms can be obtained from Dun & Bradstreet, trade associations and trade journals.

When you examine the income statement, keep in mind how you could do things differently. Be realistic about what can be changed and how fast. Know that just like an oil tanker compared to a dinghy, the larger the organization, the longer it can take to change its course.

Pro-Forma Report

Buyers look to the past to predict the future. The pro-forma report bridges that distance by anticipating the future through looking at the past. As a seller, be certain that a buyer knows that the future predictions are guesstimates not guarantees. CPAs can add the language that makes this distinction possible and frequently should be the ones to prepare these reports. Attorneys can add disclaimers. Also note that the use of pro-formas has come under greater scrutiny due to the recent accounting scandals. Although it should go without saying, as with all your documents, a pro-forma should not be used to misrepresent your financial condition. Do not fall into the trap of making one assumption a little rosier and the next one rosier still, until you end up with a document that bears no resemblance to your business. In doing so, you've created a ticking time bomb of legal liability that may explode on you at any time in the next five years or more. That's no way to get to sleep at night.

That said, the pro-forma report should include:

- two prior years of income performance

- income performance for the current year

- two years of future income performance estimates and recasted (figures that have removed unnecessary expenses to accurately reflect realistic assessments of performance, usually done by small companies to remove special expenses used to decrease net income and taxes) net income before taxes for past and future years.

A pro-forma report should be simple and it should educate. Add all the supporting documentation necessary, but keep the summary page no more than one page. Be concise. A clear and properly prepared pro-forma can mean the difference between a yea and a nay on a loan application.

A pro-forma profit and loss statement should include:

- gross profit

- labor costs

- advertising

- rent and building

- utilities, insurance and telephone

- office supplies, professional services and miscellaneous

Details from the financial statements for the five preceding years make up the bulk of the pro-forma. Still, buyers should be conservative. Erring on the low side for sales and the high side for expenses (and guessing at expenses the seller never encountered) helps you be sure you are getting sufficient value for your purchase price.

There will be some expenses the seller didn't have that need to be considered by a buyer. Aging equipment may need to be replaced, and, of course, there is the purchase price for the business the seller's statements don't include – what it's going to cost you to buy this business. In the end, the pro-forma should help you determine how much debt you can afford. Include any debt in your own pro forma calculations to see if the whole thing makes sense.

Buyers should also throw out any years with extraordinary items, since you are looking for what an average year looks like. If recent revenue looks rosy, ask yourself why. Is it the business, or a temporary economic phenomena or trend? Try not to be a buyer who buys at the top.

Cash Flow Statement

Cash on hand is necessary for any business. It is your life blood that keeps the doors open. Without it, sales and even eventual profitability cannot save you. A simple cash flow statement will show how cash moves in and out of the business over the fiscal year. This can be a simple statement (similar to a check ledger) or quite complex. Either way you should be able to tell if the company is paying out more than it is taking in. The cash flow statement is supposed to detail changes in the cash position of the company. Cash flowing out of the company (via, for example, dividends to shareholders) or cash coming into the company (from the sale of stock or the acceptance of debt) should be tracked. Beware of a situation in which the Company's "EBITDA" (Earnings Before Interest, Taxes, Depreciation and Amortization) is positive but the cash flow from operations is negative. While many people will tout a positive EBITDA, accounting trickery can easily inflate that number. The key is operating cash flow. If it is negative, the business operations aren't generating cash (as an EBITDA number may indicate) but rather eating up the company's cash. You may not want to buy a company in this condition.

Reliability: Audit vs. Unaudited Financials

Audits are as old as American capitalism itself. And by audits we don't mean the kind of tax audit you have when the IRS knocks on your door and informs you that your life is about to get miserable. Instead, the audits referred to here are the kind where an independent accounting firm comes into the business to make sure that everything is accounted for according to generally accepted accounting principles (or, "GAAP") and, in essence, that no one is cooking the books.

Audits came into being to satisfy British investors in their American businesses. The investors weren't in the neighborhood to check on their cattle ranch or railroad or timber mill, so they would hire an independent accountant to review the books and report back. The auditors' job was to represent the owner, not the management.

Similarly, the Securities and Exchange Commission requires that all public companies have audited financials. The idea is that the independent auditor will represent the true owners of a public company – the shareholders – and serve as a check against management's potential for manipulation of the books. The Enron collapse tested the independence of outside accounting firms, and stricter standards were implemented. Firms that audit can no longer also be paid for consulting or other services, activities which create a conflict of interest. (Large CPA firms are no longer faced with the dilemma of: "Do we overlook that problem in the audit in order to preserve our million dollar consulting fee?") Now, if you audit a company that's all you do.

Many smaller companies will not have audited financials prepared due to the expensive nature of the auditing process. In an audit the outside accountant basically double checks and independently verifies every transaction. If receipts or some form of documentation are not provided, that transaction cannot be audited.

A lesser form of audit is a review. In a review, the accountant doesn't audit each and every transaction, but rather reviews a select number of them to make sure that GAAP is followed. The final form is known as a compilation, in which the accountant takes the company's word that everything is okay and compiles the information.

So while an audit gives you an independent certification of all transactions and a review gives you a selected review of some of the transactions, a compilation gives you no independent investigation whatsoever.

Most businesses for sale will provide you with compilation financials. Which means you need to understand the principles in this chapter (and hopefully bring your own independent CPA onto your team) because you are going to have to do your own investigation. Still, even with audited financials prepared by the most prestigious accounting firm in town, you are going to want to conduct your own due diligence review. Trust, but verify.

Another issue arises if you are looking to buy a private company and take it public. As mentioned, in the name of investor disclosure, the SEC requires that all publicly-traded companies provided audited financials. So, if you are buying a private company with the idea of taking it public, be sure to see if the books and records are in good enough shape to withstand an outside audit. If there are gaps that can't be independently verified, you may not be able to obtain an audit. Without an audit, you can't go public.

Ideally, as a buyer, you will be looking for financials prepared by an outside CPA. When an outside accountant prepares the financials, a report letter outlining whether or not the report is audited is included. If you don't see the letter, you have no way of knowing how reliable the report is going to be. Is it a compilation? Did the outside CPA simply compile what the business owner gave them without any scrutiny or review? If the company's books have been compiled, or prepared in-house, you may want to negotiate having your own accountant go in and prepare up-to-date financials.

Analyzing Ratios

Ratios allow comparisons on a standardized basis. Ratios allow comparisons between years, between companies and between a target company and its industry.

Following are some (certainly not all) ratios to consider:

1. Liquidity ratios: ability of a company to pay its bills
   a. working capital = current assets – current liabilities
   b. current ratio = current assets/current liabilities
      above 2 is adequate, between 1 and 1.5 is low

    c. quick ratio = (cash [including cash equivalents] + accounts and notes receivable) / current liabilities

       this ratio does not include inventory

    d. sales/accounts receivable ratio = net sales / accounts and notes receivable

       shows how quickly accounts receivables are converted into cash – higher ratio means quicker turnover. To compute the amount of time a receivable is outstanding, divide the sales/accounts receivable ratio by 365

    e. stock to sales ratio = cost of goods sold / inventory

       measures the number of times inventory turns over in a year – high ratio means quick turnover. To compute the time an average item sits in inventory, divide the cost of goods sold to inventory ratio by 365

    f. solvency = (current liabilities + long-term debt) / (equity capital + total liabilities)

       measures whether or not the company is over-leveraged — should be significantly less than 1

2. Lending ratios: attractiveness to a lender

    a. coverage ratio = earnings before interest and taxes (EBIT) / annual interest expense

       high ratio means the business should be able to meet interest expenses

    b. cash flow/current maturities ratio = net profits (also known as depreciation and depletion and amortization) / current portion of long-term debt

       measures cash on hand to service the principal on debt

    c. liabilities/net worth ratio = total liabilities / tangible net worth

3. Operational and management ratios:

    a. profit/assets ratio = (profit before taxes / total assets) x 100

       the higher the percentage, the more capable a company to turn invested capital into earnings

b. net profit margin ratio = net income after tax / net sales
c. marketing cost ratio = ((total sale + marketing costs) / total sales) x 100

   percentage of sales dollar spent on sale and marketing
d. book return on equity = net income / owner's equity

   measures the amount of net income reported compared to the total equity investment by shareholders to create that net income
e. PE (price-to-earning) ratio = stock price / (12-month earnings / number of issued shares) measures the comparison between current market price of a stock and its earnings

Ratios can be compared to those of similar businesses. A good business broker will have these on hand, or you can find them yourself. Dun & Bradstreet's Industry Norms and Key Business Ratios is one resource. Getting information for previous years (five is recommended) will allow you to track trends for the target company and compare those trends to similar businesses as well.

Remember, all the financial data tells you is how things have been in the past. It can offer guidance as to how you can change the business to increase profits, but it does not predict the future.

Also note the advice of billionaire financier Warren Buffet. The rule for Mr. Buffett, one of the most successful investors of all time, is that if you don't know how a company makes its money don't buy into it. You need to know that accounting can obfuscate and deflect. Accounting can be a professional form of smoke and mirrors. Unless you have a clear sighted understanding of the workings of the company's financials, you're better off just not getting involved.

Rich Dad's Tips

- Don't get involved with a seller who won't or can't provide complete financial information.

- A profit on paper may not be a profit in reality. You may need to dig deep to fully understand a company's financials.

- Be sure to analyze a company's accounts receivables. The information gained will tell you a lot about the business.

As well, you must clearly comprehend the company's ...

Chapter Eight

Liabilities

Case No. 8 – Morgan and Gordon

Morgan owned an auto body and painting business on the older, east side of town. Morgan's Auto Body & Paints, Inc., had always done well, in part because Morgan was attractive and charming and she knew how to treat the insurance adjusters and car lot owners who sent a lot of business her way.

After many years of building up the business, Morgan wanted to retire to Maui, Key West, or some other tropical locale, and so she put the body shop up for sale.

After several months of being quietly on the market, Gordon showed up to take a close look at Morgan's Auto Body & Paint, Inc. He was intrigued. Morgan had a good reputation in town for keeping costs down and getting work in and out the door. She had kept the equipment new and the shop clean. The only downside for Gordon was that the building she owned was in a older industrial area of town, away from the path of new growth to the west. But when he discussed it with her, Morgan was very persuasive about the importance of the building. First of all, she stated that all of the adjusters and her other referral sources knew where it was. It was an easy and comfortable location for them. Secondly, she noted that an industrial business like hers was not likely to get zoning for the west side of town anyway. And thirdly, she said that the building was part of the sale price, which, she pointed out, was to Gordon's advantage. It was always better to be a landlord than a tenant.

Gordon mulled over the deal, which started to make sense. He could come up with the financing to purchase both the business and the building, but he couldn't really afford an attorney to help him with all the paperwork. He searched the internet, found an asset purchase agreement, and filled it in on his own.

When he presented the agreement to Morgan she wanted to tweak it. Instead of buying the assets – the equipment, the building and all – she wanted Gordon to buy the stock in Morgan's Auto Body & Paint, Inc. She explained that it was a much cleaner deal that way. The assets were already held and titled in the name of Morgan's Auto Body & Paint, Inc. They wouldn't have the hassle and cost of having to retitle everything into the name of Gordon's corporation. In fact, she noted, Gordon wouldn't even have to pay to form a new corporation, since he would be using her existing one.

Morgan also said on her end she would pay less taxes on a sale of corporate shares. Since she had held the shares for over a year the tax rate (at this writing) was only a 15% capital gains rate. If they did an asset sale she would have to pay recapture (at higher tax rates) for all the depreciation she had taken on the equipment. And since she would pay less in taxes with a stock sale Morgan offered Gordon a $10,000 discount on the sales price if the handled it that way.

Gordon was very interested in saving on any legal expenses. It made sense to use Morgan's corporation rather than spending the money to form a new one. And he liked getting a $10,000 discount on the sales price.

So the agreement was changed from an asset purchase agreement to a stock purchase agreement. Instead of buying the assets – the equipment, the customers and the goodwill – from the corporation, Gordon bought directly from Morgan the shares of Morgan's corporation, which owned all of the same assets anyway.

A chart illustrates the differences between an asset sale and a stock sale:

Asset Sale

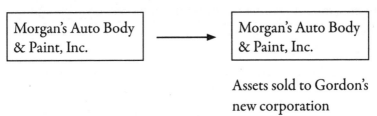

Assets sold to Gordon's
new corporation

Stock Sale

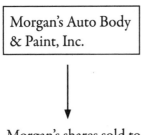

Morgan's shares sold to
Gordon. Assets stay in
corporation.

The sale went through and Gordon acquired Morgan's corporation. Morgan took her money and moved to Belize.

A month later the government's environmental authorities showed up at the auto body shop. A review indicated that for over 15 years the business had been unlawfully disposing of hazardous wastes into a covered sump in the back. The paint, oil and other foul solvents had severely contaminated the groundwater in the area. A multi-million dollar remediation project would be necessary. Under the strict liability CERCLA rules, the corporation was responsible.

Gordon protested vehemently. He hadn't dumped hazardous wastes anywhere. He didn't even know about the covered sump out back. It wasn't his fault the groundwater was contaminated. The EPA official politely and firmly suggested that Gordon contact an attorney.

When Gordon finally met with an attorney he learned the hard truth. By buying stock in Morgan's corporation, he not only bought all of the corporation's assets, but all of its liabilities as well. The fact that Gordon hadn't dumped hazardous waste anywhere didn't matter. He was the sole owner of a corporation that had done so and thus he was responsible.

The attorney then explained that if the transaction been an asset sale instead of a stock sale, the whole thing could have been avoided. If Gordon had bought the business' assets and moved them to another location, like he had wanted to do in the first place, he would not have been responsible. This is because the general rule is that when you purchase the assets from an entity you do not become liable for the debts and liabilities of that entity. But when you purchase the entity, as in Gordon's case in which he bought Morgan's corporation, you acquire not only all of the assets but all of the liabilities as well.

The attorney told Gordon that he would have a claim against Morgan for misrepresentation on the sale and for contribution on the environmental remediation project. But she had disappeared into Belize. Suing her and then collecting from her would be extremely difficult, if not impossible. Gordon was ruined.

As Gordon's case illustrates, there are many liabilities to be concerned about when you buy and sell a business. It is important to understand whether you are acquiring assets only (without any attendant liabilities) as in an asset sale, or if the liabilities become yours, as in a stock purchase agreement.

The General Rule of Successor Liability holds that when a new company, which we'll call "Newco," purchases the assets of an existing company, known as "Oldco," the debts and liabilities stay with Oldco. However, as exceptions to this General Rule, Newco may become liable when:

1. The transaction is really a merger, in which the seller continues as an absorbed part of the buyer and the seller's officers and owners continue their roles.

2. There is an express or implied assumption of liability, meaning that Newco agreed to pick up some debt. A court may (or may not) extend such assumption to all debts.

3. The transaction was fraudulent. If a court found that the intent was to strip Oldco of its assets and leave it exposed to all the liabilities with no money to pay them, the court may find that Newco participated in a fraudulent transaction. Factors to be considered will be whether there is common ownership between Newco and Oldco, whether Newco actually paid money for the assets and whether the same people are being used to make the same product in the same location. While no one factor is determinative, if the whole transfer doesn't pass the smell test, Newco may be held liable for Oldco's debts.

If you are buying assets and the protective General Rule of Successor Liability does not apply, or if you are buying the stock of a company and know that liabilities will continue, what are some of the liabilities to look out for?

1. Hazardous Waste. As in Gordon's case, this is a huge and potentially devastating issue to be dealt with. Federal law basically holds four classes of parties responsible for clean up of a hazardous waste site:
   a. The current owner and operator of the business property;
   b. The owner and operator of the business property at the time the waste was deposited;
   c. Those who generated the waste and sent it to the site; and
   d. Those who transported waste to the site.

The liability is "strict liability," which means that in a court case all the government has to do to win is prove that there is waste on the site. It is that simple. If there is waste on the site the owner is liable. Whatever your excuse for why it is there is of absolutely no use. The dog ate my environmental plan won't work, nor will any sane and reasonable explanations. You are just guilty, period, end of story.

So how do you protect yourself? If you have the slightest inkling, suspicion or concern that hazardous waste could be an issue, you may want to have a Phase I environmental report prepared. There are state-licensed engineers who will come out to a property and or a business and do a survey of potential environmental problems. If no problems appear they will say so in a written report. If a concern shows up, they may suggest that a more in-depth report, a Phase II environmental report, be prepared. If a clean report can't be obtained, you will obviously reconsider buying the business. That is, unless you relish the thought, as in Gordon's case, of you and your family some day out of the blue being thrown into the vortex of immediate financial ruin.

Whatever you do, save those reports. If, for example, you get a clean Phase I report and you go ahead and buy the business, that document may protect you into the future. Within the federal law there is the "innocent landowner defense." It requires a purchaser to prove that at the time of acquisition they "did not know and had no reason to know that any hazardous substance ... was disposed of, on, in or at the facility." (42 U.S.C. §9601 (35)(A)(i)). The fact that you intended to comply with the environmental laws by having an engineer check out the property before your purchase and the property was reported as clear is a very good argument to have.

Appendix B contains a checklist of suggested environment documents and records to be reviewed prior to purchasing a business.

2. Accounts Payable. The accounts payable of a business are the monies that are owed to others, for rent, supplies and the like. In simplest terms, accounts payable liabilities are claims on a business' assets. Short of bankruptcy, cash or items converted to cash must be used to settle these claims. As a buyer, you want to look at how much a company owes, but you also want to look a little deeper. Who has the claims against assets? What kinds of expenses are common for the business? A balance sheet isn't enough. Be sure to get an accounts payable analysis from the seller as well. With such numbers in hand, consider:

- the terms of liabilities

- specific information on suppliers

- timeliness of debt payments

- collection status of debts

- status of any loans

- interest rates and terms of any loans

- company credit rating

- status of tax obligations

Remember that these aren't just details on paper. They are not just the seller's problem. As soon as you sign a stock purchase agreement, and in some cases, an asset purchase agreement, all these liabilities become yours. It is prudent to understand what it all means to you.

Some sellers will want to sell a buyer stock rather than assets because of accounts payable (or other!) liabilities about which they don't want buyers to know. As we've discussed, this may not be the best way to proceed. However, if a stock sale is the way it has to be structured, a buyer may want to insist upon an indemnification and escrow clause. In this scenario, a part of the purchase price is left in an escrow account administered by an independent party. The seller indemnifies the buyer against any pre-existing claims. If unknown claims are later asserted against the business, monies are paid from the escrow account to satisfy them. After a set period of time (i.e. 6 months, one year, etc.), any remaining monies in the escrow are then forwarded to the seller. Such a procedure can give the buyer some comfort that he or she won't be entirely responsible for a torrent of unknown claims. Some sales agreements may even provide that if the claims exceed the escrow amount the seller must pay a penalty, or the seller must give the buyers their money back and retake the business, or something similar to protect the buyer.

Many buyers will be aware of the bulk sales laws, the intent of which is to protect creditors. Prior to an entity sale, notice of the intended sale is to be sent to known creditors, published in a local newspaper and recorded with the county recorder and/or secretary of state. Failure to follow the rules could mean that the buyer would become responsible for the seller's accounts payable.

A number of states, including Nevada, have repealed their bulk sales laws. While noble in its intent, the bulk sales process was a clunky, slowing anchor that benefited lawyers more than creditors or businesses. Still, some states have the bulk sales rules in place, so be sure to check with yes – I know – your lawyer to see if it applies to you.

3. Products Liability. Over the last hundred years the doctrine of "caveat emptor," or "buyer beware," has given way to, it can be argued, a more sensible public policy whereby companies bear responsibility for the defective products they put into the marketplace. After all, in terms of fairness, who is better at getting cost-effective product liability insurance coverage, the consumer who buys one thermonuclear hedge trimmer, or the company that makes a million of them? And similarly, who is in a better position to ensure their safety, a consumer using one, or a manufacturer producing many?

So, the question regarding product liability becomes, does the General Rule of Successor Liability apply when one entity sells its assets to another? Does a mere purchase of assets mean that product liability claims will not follow?

The short answer is yes. Such claims will not follow. The product liability laws do not alter the General Rule. However, where the selling entity is dissolved, liability of the buying entity may be governed by state laws to the contrary. So be sure to check your local rules when purchasing such assets.

As well, there is a "product line exception" to the General Rule. In a situation where:

a) The buyer publicly holds itself out as a continuation of the seller and produces the same product under a similar name;
b) The buyer acquires substantially all of the seller's assets; and
c) The buyer benefits from the seller's goodwill

Some courts, most notably California, will impose strict liability on the buyer for defects in products made by the seller.

The justification for this exception to the General Rule is fairness. In buying all of the seller's assets the buyer extinguished an injured party's product liability remedies and yet was deemed to have the ability to assume the original manufacturer's role in spreading risk through insurance. Courts have held that the party who can bear the risk and is benefiting from the seller's original goodwill, in all fairness, should have continuing responsibility for such claims.

The key for buyers then is insurance. If you are buying the assets of a manufacturing company and will continue producing the same product under a similar name, make sure you have the product liability insurance in place to not only cover future claims on your products but also any additional claims on the seller's previously manufactured products.

4. Labor Law

    In the case of a stock sale, relations with union member employees will not change. However, in the case of an asset sale, the buyer, as a general rule, is not bound by the seller's collective bargaining agreements. If the buyer does not agree to assume a contract, he or she is not responsible for its terms. Of course, this will not help matters if the buyer is planning to try and retain company employees, although some employees may prefer not to pay the union dues. You'll need to weigh the advantages and disadvantages of assuming such an agreement.

    Also note that the National Labor Relations Board may determine the sale of assets is a ploy to get out of a labor agreement and seek to have the buyer comply with the agreement anyway. This occurs when there is substantial continuity (i.e., similar businesses, employees, products, working conditions and customers) between the old and new employer. Again, you'll need to analyze your position before attending your first gentle, rational and unemotional labor negotiation.

5. Tax Liabilities

    When sellers sell their business, governments, like other creditors, prefer to get paid then and there. So, unlike other creditors, they put laws in place to ensure that they'll get their tax money.

As a general rule, taxes are the responsibility of the business that incurred the liability. But that doesn't stop the government from using the buyer to make sure the seller pays. For example, in Nevada the purchaser is required to withhold a portion of the purchase price in order to cover any sales, property, unemployment or other taxes that are due. Failure to do so can mean personal liability for the buyer on the taxes owed by the seller.

A common way to handle such tax obligations is to get a tax clearance certificate issued by the appropriate governmental authorities. The certificate certifies that the applicable taxes have been paid. It is frequently an item handled by an escrow agent pursuant to escrow instructions. As mentioned, as a buyer you will want to make certain that these taxes are paid so that you don't incur personal liability for them later.

Rich Dad's Tips

*   If a seller insists upon a stock sale be sure to consult with a lawyer as to the consequences.

*   Don't be swayed by a sales price discount for accepting a stock sale. That discount will evaporate if there are later problems.

*   If you are buying a company that has used any chemical or solvent in its business, no matter how insignificant, consider obtaining an environmental report.

*   Be sure to analyze the ability and cost of obtaining products liability insurance when buying a manufacturing company.

With the financials and liabilities understood, next we need to understand ...

Chapter Nine

Valuation

Case No. 9 – Tommy and Vinny

Tommy had worked hard all his life. He had saved enough money while working two jobs and providing for his family to begin looking at buying his own business.

Tommy was great with people. He was a storyteller and a natural motivator. His wife and family felt that if he ever found the right business to fit his outgoing and genuine personality, he would be successful.

The issue was: What was the right business for Tommy? And once that was answered, he needed to consider whether he could afford such a business.

Tommy started by going to a business expo to learn about franchise opportunities. He had read that franchises were one of the safest businesses to start because the failure rate was lower than that of other, non-franchise, start-ups. He read that an advantage was the franchisor and previous franchisees had already made all the start-up mistakes so that his learning curve would be easier.

But in considering the franchise opportunities at the expo, Tommy was struck by two things. First, the franchise fees that the franchisors wanted were significant. Many tens of thousands of dollars was required to start followed by a continuing monthly royalty paid in perpetuity. Of course, Tommy acknowledged that if the right franchise made you the right amount of money, it would all be worth it.

But that was the second issue. Tommy didn't see the right franchise. He wasn't going to be a carpet cleaner, sandwich maker or locksmith. There was nothing wrong with those businesses. It was just that Tommy (and his family) knew he had to find the right business for his personality if he was going to succeed. They knew they only had the once chance with the money they had struggled to save, and their choice had to be the right one.

So Tommy kept looking. He read the business opportunity section of his local paper and spoke with local business brokers. He had never known there were so many businesses available for consideration.

Still, Tommy didn't find the right business. By now, he was getting restless. He had continued to work two jobs but wanted to get on with his own business. He thought about quitting both jobs to focus on the business search. His wife calmed him down. Because they absolutely had to make a once-in-a-lifetime correct decision, there was no need to rush it.

Then she had an idea that, at first, seemed crazy.

She suggested that Tommy talk to her second cousin, Vinny, a psychologist at a state college three hours north. Tommy thought it was crazy. He didn't need a shrink to tell him what business to get into. Vinny wasn't a shrink, his wife explained. Vinny was a Ph.D., not an MD, and he dealt with personality issues rather than psychiatric disorders. And for Tommy, the right business had to be tied to his personality, which, she gently reminded him, was a very good one.

So, Tommy met with Vinny, who, as Tommy recalled as they sat down, was a pretty good guy. Vinny said that he had gone through this exercise before with many of his clients and it was something he enjoyed because it helped entrepreneurs find the right business for them.

Vinny called it "occupational therapy" because it provided guidance to people who weren't happy with their careers and needed a major change. It was a systematic way of finding out what business was best for him all the way around, both emotionally and practically. Tommy shifted in his chair.

Vinny explained that there were three factors he needed to consider: 1) Tommy's personality and interests, 2) his aptitudes and skills, and 3) financial and practical aspects of his situation.

"The first thing we need to do Vinny said is to evaluate your personality and interests. I call this 'looking into your heart' because this where you get a chance to set aside all of your financial and practical worries and think about what you really want for your professional life. If you could own any business in the world, what would it be?"

Tommy sighed heavily and Vinny could see his brow furrow as he pondered the question. It was as if he hadn't ever allowed himself the luxury of thinking about it in such an impractical way. After all, he'd considered a franchised business, which, in effect was *someone else's*. After awhile, Tommy's brow unfurrowed, and he sat up. "I really enjoy dealing with people, and I like sales, but what I want most is to sell people things that they're going to value and appreciate, maybe even take pride in."

"That sounds good," said Vinny, as he wrote on his notepad. "Now I want you to tell me what you're best at. Think of all the jobs you've had and how you did in school, and tell me what skills set you apart from most other people. If you can't think of any, I can give you a test that might tease out some of those skills."

This time Tommy didn't need time to think, "I've always had the gift of gab. Take for example when I was in Little League, I sold more raffle tickets than any other kid in the league because I could make adults laugh. Even though I was nine years old, I could sell like a middle-aged car salesman, and they loved it. Plus I enjoyed it because I felt like I was accomplishing something worthwhile. All that money went into buying our uniforms."

Vinny looked up from his notepad. "It's great that you know yourself so well. Most people I talk to have a difficult time figuring out what skills they have. Usually I have to administer an occupational aptitude test." Vinny looked down again, "Now, one last question. As far as your finances and personal life are concerned, what kind of business do you think you can handle?"

"I'm not really sure what you mean," replied Tommy. "Are you talking about the size of it, or what kind of thing I'm selling."

"Both. Tell me how much of an investment you can afford to put into it, and how big you want it to be."

"Well," said Tommy, "with a loan from the bank and what I have in savings, I can afford to put about $50,000 into it. And as for the size, I want to keep it small. Maybe someone to answer the phones and one other person."

When the interview and process had been completed, Tommy and Vinny had come up with a business that Tommy was genuinely excited about.

Tommy was going to sell advertising specialties – pens, coffee mugs, t-shirts and the like, imprinted with the company's name. It was a competitive business, but Tommy was ebullient, gregarious and a natural salesman. He already knew a lot of people in town who could use his services. And, based on the 80/20 rule, where 80% of the business is done by the top 20% of the salesman, at the top end, where Tommy fully intended to be, a salesman could make over $250,000 a year.

All Tommy had to do now was to decide whether to buy an advertising specialties franchise or start one himself. The franchise opportunities looked interesting, and for some people they would be the right way to go, but Tommy didn't want to be restrained by many franchisor's territorial restrictions. He wanted to sell to anyone, anywhere.

And so Tommy started his own advertising specialties business. And it was a huge success.

As many of you have already figured out by now, the point of this story is that there are many ways to value a business, and we'll get into a number of formulaic methods in a minute. But before you ever place a dollar value on a business, you've got to value it for what it is for you: It should be a provider, and hopefully a blessing. Like a child, it will be an overwhelming commitment and an extension of yourself. It will shape how others see you, and how you see yourself. It is important to recognize these values at the start.

The purpose here is to slow down that train as it gathers speed to make a decision. A decision must be made, yes. But it must be made in due course and after thoughtful consideration. Remember our case with Paul, Victoria and Danny, and the GrillKing business? The rush to move forward absolutely had to be tempered with a hard, cold analysis of the financials. Similarly, in our case with Tommy, the rush to decide must be tempered with a very personal valuation analysis. Many people only get one chance to start a business. And many will remain in that business for the rest of their days. Given the continuing importance of the decision, the valuation analysis – the very personal procedure of valuing a business – is crucial.

Alright, now that our reality check is complete, let's cautiously move forward. You have decided on a personal level that a certain business is of value for you. How do you decide on a dollar value for that business?

Businesses don't come with handy price tags, consumer reports or easily accessed comparisons. Putting a value on a business is, at best, in inexact science. Yet, coming up with a value to paste on the company may be the most important step in the acquisition process. Sellers need to set a price that will attract interest. Buyers need to know if that price is fair.

Buyers: While your accountant can be a valuable resource, you should at least understand how to value a business on your own. That way, you can do some preliminary calculations on your own and start separating the keepers from the losers.

It is important to remember that a business really has only three things to sell: assets, the potential of those assets to produce earnings and goodwill, the rather intangible value of being in business. While buying a business is an investment involving risk, the question to answer is whether the investment you are about to make will bring better returns than other investments. Is your money better off in the bank, in the stock market or in real estate? Or can you get a better return, with perhaps more risk, by purchasing a business? Combined with answering those questions is the interrelated issue of valuing the target company. If the valuation is too high the buyer sees less of a return. Ultimately it all comes down to what you are willing to spend.

But in the world of business brokerage there are valuation methods used to quantify the very inexact science of valuing a business. These are rules of thumb guesstimates that certain professionals will use in the same manner as an immutable law of physics. Do not be swayed by a business broker who insists that the hard and fast asset approach indicates the company is worth exactly $1 million. If you are only willing to pay $750,000 for the business, then that's the only valuation method you need to know. Don't let anyone else tell you otherwise. This is not to denigrate the efforts of professional appraisers who in most cases seek to arrive at a fair and reasonable number. It is rather to give you the knowledge that valuations are opinions, not facts, and that your opinion is the most important one.

Because these valuation methods get thrown around so much it is important to know what they are about, if only to poke holes in them to your advantage. The following is a quick review.

Approaches to value are based on the following appraisal principles, which are useful to remember when negotiating.

- The Principle of Future Benefits: Economic value reflects anticipated future benefits.

- The Principle of Substitution: Parties have the choice of an equally desirable substitute.

- The Principle of Alternatives: Each party in every type of transaction has alternatives to consummating the transaction.

Remember how we have discussed that if the deal doesn't feel right you should get up and walk away from it? That act demonstrates the Principle of Alternatives at work.

From the principles above, approaches to value have evolved.

The Market (Comparison) Approach: As the name suggests, this approach deals with the fair market value of the business – the price a similarly sized company in a similar industry would garner when a willing seller meets a willing and able buyer. But no two businesses are alike, thus the problem. Accurate comparisons are difficult at best, impossible at worst. And even if adequately similar companies did exist, and even if they did sell in an adequate time frame, there's no databank of such sales available.

The Asset Approach: If a company has a lot of hard assets that can be sold, this is a popular method of valuation. It assumes the business' value is equal to the value of the assets, which, of course, can be inaccurate. Nearly every business has intangible values (customer lists, location, non-compete covenants, etc.), which are not considered in the asset approach. By not taking into account any future ability of the assets and intangibles to generate income, the method is suspect.

Net Adjusted Asset Approach: For more accuracy than afforded by the straight Asset Approach, value the assets, liabilities and intangibles, then subtract the value of the liabilities from the value of the assets and add the value of the intangibles.

The Earnings Approach: The most widely used method is the earnings approach, which, pursuant to the Principle of Future Benefits, measures the worth of earnings. From this approach have sprung three separate valuation methodologies. They are:

1. Capitalization of Earnings: This technique places value on the company's potential to earn money (using a capitalization rate), with assets as incidental to that potential. For calculation purposes, assume future earnings will be the same as the past (go back at least three to five years). List the tax profits for each year and multiply by a capitalization rate to get the company value. The difficult part of this method is finding the best capitalization rate for the target company. The buyer or their accountant will need to do some research to find the most accurate rate to use, which is usually in the range of eight percent to fourteen percent.

2. Discounted Cash Flow: The goal here is to determine the amount of money today that would equal all the future money you can expect to receive. As with the capitalization of earnings method, this technique considers earnings for valuation. But whereas the capitalization method uses historical data, the discounted cash flow method uses projected future earnings (usually for a three- to ten-year period). Future profitability calculations require consideration of how a buyer can or will change the business. Reduction of expenses, increase of advertising and the like need to be thought through. Then projected earnings are discounted at a specific rate.

Here's where it gets tricky: choosing the discount rate. The rate is usually chosen with consideration to the return required on the assets, degree of risk, and equity and debt levels. This is a complex process and should not be done without advice from a professional with experience in such valuations.

3. Ratio Multiplier (industry rules of thumb): Each industry has a formula that can be applied to it as a rule of thumb for a ballpark valuation figure. These multipliers consider sales, but not profits and can be found with industry associations or at the reference desk of your local library. The use of multipliers is a quite simplistic (and often inaccurate) method of finding a company's value. However, it can be useful when taking a quick first glance at a seller's price, especially in terms of service businesses where it is most often used.

4. The IRS-Recommended Approach: The IRS suggests you:
   1. Determine average annual return on tangible assets (for a period of not less than five years). If no history is available, assume a rate of eight percent to ten percent.
   2. Determine average earnings for the preceding five years.
   3. Subtract returns from earnings. This is the amount attributable to intangibles, such as goodwill, which is the value of the business that is above and beyond the value of the assets.
   4. Capitalize at a rate of 10 percent to 20 percent for high-risk businesses, 8 percent to 15 percent for low risk businesses.
   5. Add the goodwill results to the book value of assets.

However, this method (established in 1968) is considered to be outdated by some and tends to overvalue businesses. Still, the IRS suggests buyers always consider the following:

- nature and history of the business
- economic environment for overall economy and specific industry
- book value, financial condition and earning capacity
- capacity to pay dividends

- intangible value
- prior sales of company stock
- market price for similar businesses

Appraisers: With cooperation from the seller, a buyer may want to bring in a professional business appraiser. The process may take a while (several weeks at a minimum) and cost a bit ($5,000 to $15,000 or more), but it does provide objectivity. A good local appraiser will have a handle on what values are in your local market.

Seller's Side

When it comes to valuation, many sellers let emotion get the best of them. In fact, many fail to understand exactly what makes up the value of a company. As a seller, you may be viewing the value of your company based on what you think it might do in the future. But your knowledge of the future comes from how you do things. A buyer is a whole different breed and may not be capable of reproducing your results, nor may he or she want to. What you haven't done holds little or no value to a buyer. If you think changes will increase the value of the company, do them before the sale.

On the other hand, past performance does have an intangible value that can increase or decrease the value of hard assets. Better than average past performance will bring the value of the company proportionately higher.

Be sure you are not rationalizing your price right out of the market. Price should be based on a number of factors and emotion is not one of them. It is human nature to rationalize, and more than one seller has let rationalization rule over professional advice and sometimes even common sense.

Buyer's Side

As we have said, don't rely on what the seller or business broker tells you about a business, especially when it comes to value. The seller may hand you an appraisal, hoping you will take it at face value. Don't. Involve your professional team in the process. You may want to use all the valuation methods above as a sort of check and double-check to see if a price seems fair. Members of your team, having no financial stake in the price (unlike the seller and/or the seller's business broker) are good sounding boards for your ideas and decisions.

Keep in mind that most initial asking prices for a company are on the high side. Sellers fully expect negotiations to bring down the price. However, if the seller has employed a professional to perform the valuation analysis, the asking price is more likely to be realistic and may not have as much wiggle room. Still, the gap between initial price and selling price tends to be between ten percent and twenty-five percent. In some cases it may be more, thus underscoring the importance of understanding the market for such businesses.

Goodwill

It is indeed incredible that one of the most common terms involved in buying and selling a business is one of the hardest to pin down.

Goodwill can be defined as the assessable value of being in business for a period of time. In the heat of negotiations, goodwill may also be viewed by a seller as the profit to be made over and above the cost of fixtures and equipment for sticking with the business for so many years. Likewise, goodwill may be viewed by the buyer as a business's inflated view of self-worth, ranging from unrealistic to delusional, that must be negotiated downward to make the deal work.

So what is goodwill? From an accounting standpoint it is the difference between the purchase price and the appraised value of the assets. If you pay $5 million dollars for a business and the fixtures, furniture and equipment are appraised at $3 million, you've paid $2 million for the goodwill of the company. You've paid $2 million for the fact that 1) the company has been in business for a period of time, and 2) combining the assets you bought with the fact of being in business provides a means of generating revenues.

So how does one precisely value the benefits of being in business and generating revenues? How many angels can dance on the head of a pin?

Do not trouble yourself with calculating and over-analyzing goodwill as a fixed number. Instead, treat it as the remainder in a shifting subtraction problem. Purchase Price minus Value of Assets equals Goodwill. If you decrease the asset price without changing the purchase price your goodwill will be higher. The issue generally will center around the relationship between the purchase price and goodwill. Once the assets have been valued, what are you willing to pay for the goodwill of being in business? The lower the goodwill price, the lower the purchase price.

Sellers will argue that the ability to generate revenues, the fact of being in business with doors open and customers clamoring, is a valuable and hard to replicate asset. Buyers will argue the Principle of Alternatives. The alternative exists to start one's own business or to purchase a smaller, similar business. As such, goodwill represents the value of not hassling with a start-up and being further along with the enterprise. For buyers, goodwill represents convenience, not a kingdom.

How goodwill is ultimately valued will be dynamically determined in negotiations. So remember, it is not a fixed number. Politely disagree with the seller/lawyer/broker who tells you it is.

Operational Investigation

As a buyer, you'll need to understand all the ins and outs of a target business. It's not enough that the price is right. In order for the deal to be a good one, you will need to be intimately familiar with the company – its past, present and future. You'll want to know all about risks, all about taxes and all about operations.

The operational investigation is the key to your understanding of the target firm. In fact, it should even precede the financial analysis. No two businesses are alike, so you will need to customize the list of questions to your industry and your needs. While a more complete checklist is found at Appendix A, the following information is most certainly needed:

1. Who owns the company? Find out which corporate entity the company is operating under and the names of shareholders, if applicable.

2. What does the company sell? This sounds like a softball, but many companies have more than one source of revenue. You need to know and understand all sales and what percentage of revenues each category represents, whether each category is increasing or decreasing, and when products or services were added or are planned to be added.

3. Will products or services be affected by technological changes?

4. Are products or services protected from competitors? Check if there are any patents, trademarks or copyrights and if they are owned and transferable.

5. How does the product or service rate when compared to others in the industry? If the industry is regulated by government (federal or state) entities, reports may be available.

6. Who are the customers? You want to understand demographics, how many customers support the business and at what percentage of sales, rate of reorders and repeat business, payment histories, contract terms and whether or not customers are likely to remain after a change in ownership.

7. What kind of credit does the company extend to customers?

8. What are current marketing, advertising and PR efforts? You'll want information on the success or failure of such efforts, target markets, future plans, budget, in-house and outside contributions and those ever-helpful comparisons to industry norms.

9. Does the company have exclusivity with reference to production or distribution rights?

10. Who is the competition? Include information about number of competitors; competitive structure of the industry; advertising, marketing and PR promotions; trends of competitors; and future changes. Remember our case with Hank, Kent and the Taiwanese

injection molding upheaval. Be sure to consider all possible and even remote forms of future competition.

11. Who are the suppliers? Find out about the company's relationship with suppliers, its reputation, number of suppliers, how much the company relies on each, the conditions of the supplier's industry and payment terms.

12. Who is in management? Include how involved the owner is, how important any key employees may be, agreements (such as non-compete agreements), and relationships with personnel.

13. Who are the employees? You'll want to know how critical current employees are, whether or not they are likely to stay on after a change in ownership, terms of employment contracts and/or collective bargaining agreements, depth of the local labor market compared to the company's needs, contents of employee or operations manuals, status and skills of supervisors, employee relationships with customers, employee relationships with management and owners, compensation terms, benefit terms, payroll procedures, hiring and firing practices, raise and promotion practices, productivity of current staff, comparison to industry norms for compensation and terms, and any training programs available.

14. What is the location? Pay special attention to the facility and lease. Include information on neighborhood trends, proper use of the space, adequacy of the facility, terms of lease, expansion possibilities and needs, and zoning restrictions.

15. Are there any tax, insurance or legal actions pending.

As buyers go through the valuation process they may want to be coy about the asking price. Certainly some may want to engage in a little posturing. Consider using the Principle of Substitution by noting you are reviewing a similar business for sale. Evoke the Principle of Future Benefits by observing that the numbers must make sense or your wife and family will disown you.

For all your posturing though, it may be strategically useful to make the seller wait on what price is acceptable to you. Your first comment on the asking price should come upon submitting a written offer to buy the business. This step conveys a seriousness of intent and a seriousness as to what you as the buyer are willing to accept. In theater it is called a dramatic entrance. In your dealings you want the effect to be the same.

The offer should contain all the terms of your proposal. Price is meaningless without terms, so don't do yourself the disservice of separating the two.

Rich Dad's Tips

- Remember that your personal valuation of the business is more important than any formula concocted by a seller or appraiser.

- Goodwill has been considered a value that decreased over time, and was thus amortized to account for such reduction in value. Recently, new accounting standards have been implemented whereby certain goodwill is viewed as remaining intact, unless somehow impaired, thus limiting amortization. Be sure to check with your CPA regarding the treatment of goodwill for accounting purposes.

- Check on the Securities & Exchange Commission's website (www.sec.gov) for companies with similar businesses to the one you are looking at. Review the securities filings, and see what these companies are reporting about the market, profits, consumer trends. There is valuable information to be had, and it doesn't cost anything to obtain.

With an offer ready, it is time for the real negotiations to begin ...

Chapter Ten

Negotiations

Case No. 10 – Pam, John and Brendan

Pam owned a lower-level minor league baseball franchise in southern Indiana. The team was well-managed and was always competitive on the field. Loyal fans were proud of the players who had gone on to excellence in the major leagues. The stadium had amenities and other attractions that made it a favorite for family entertainment over a seven-county region. Pam had benefited from the increase in popularity of minor league baseball in general and from her concentrated marketing efforts to make the game a fun, family event.

Pam had inherited the franchise from her father and had built it up over the years. Although she regretted reaching her decision, it was now time to sell. Her lawyer, Brendan, had assumed the role of general manager over the years. Brendan loved the stature that being GM of the team gave him in the community. And the job was certainly more enjoyable than practicing law. He was disappointed that Pam was selling the team.

John was a well-known local car dealer with five dealerships throughout the area. He had played in the minor leagues himself and was a lifelong baseball fan. He was greatly interested in buying the team. On a business level, he felt that there were many marketing tie-ins between his dealerships and the franchise. On a very personal level, owning a minor league baseball team would be very satisfying, the fulfillment of a lifelong dream.

Pam knew this. She and John were friends. He had mentioned on several occasions that if she ever wanted to sell he would be very, very interested in buying. Given this, Pam felt she already had a leg up on the negotiations.

The first step was to see if baseball would accept John as an owner. Professional baseball, from the majors to the minors, is a close-knit fraternity. If you are not going to fit in, the powers that be will simply refuse to approve a transfer of the franchise. No reasons are needed, although they can range from having a bad business reputation to consistent use of a hideous hairpiece. But John had a good reputation and was proudly bald. He was definitely one of the boys. Baseball gave Pam a green light to negotiate with him.

John and Pam agreed that their lawyers would conduct the negotiations. John scheduled a time for his lawyers, the two name partners of Boyden & Christensen, P.C., to meet with Brendan, the GM and counsel for the franchise.

John and Pam had already each consulted with their respective accountants as to a value for the team. The attorneys were charged with negotiating the best price as well as other issues including terms of payment.

But when they met, the attorneys couldn't get anywhere near a price. No one wanted to offer an opening price for fear of making a misstep: as a seller, being too low on price, and as a buyer, being too high on price. After several hours of posturing that turned into several fruitless meetings and several thousand dollars in attorneys' fees, Pam got fed up and directed Brendan to submit an opening offer.

At the next meeting of the three lawyers, Brendan's offer immediately offended Boyden and Christensen. How could Pam ask so much money for a business whose growth potential was nonexistent? It was a totally ridiculous number. Boyden was so incensed he got up and walked out of the room. Brendan saw it for what it was: a show. But then Christensen started talking about how his partner could be hot-headed in these things, but that the two of them could easily work things out. At this, Brendan blew up. He accused Christensen of using the oldest gambit in the book:

good cop/bad cop. He wasn't going to fall into that utterly transparent trap. Did they think he was an idiot? Brendan fumed. He got up and walked out.

The parties didn't talk again for weeks. Boyden and Christensen told John how they were playing hardball (so to speak) on his behalf. They weren't going to let John pay a penny more for the franchise than it was worth. They were also crowing to others in their circle of how tough they were playing the negotiations, with the intent that this would filter out and would improve their reputations as attorneys around town.

For his part, Brendan told Pam that John, through Boyden and Christensen, was trying to steal the team. He assured Pam that he wasn't going to let that happen. He was her attorney and general manager and he would protect her interests, whether the team sold or not.

There was something about the way Brendan made that last statement that concerned Pam. She wondered whether his interest in remaining as general manager of the team was more important to him than in representing her in a successful sale.

A week later Pam ran into John at a chamber mixer. After an initial awkwardness, they spoke again as friends. Pam confided to John that perhaps Brendan wasn't too keen on seeing the team sold. She knew he greatly enjoyed being the team's general manager and perhaps the prospect of being replaced was affecting his negotiations.

John then responded that perhaps his attorneys weren't helping the process either. He had heard through the grapevine that some were saying Boyden & Christensen were using the transaction to improve their local standing as hard-nosed negotiators. John was angry that his lawyers would waste his money and ignore his objectives in order to build their own reputations.

Pam and John had a laugh at the absurdity of allowing the foxes to rule the henhouse. Over another drink they reached a deal as to price, terms and conditions for the sale of the franchise. They each hired a new attorney from outside the area to complete the necessary paperwork.

The lesson here is that if you are going to let other people negotiate for you, be certain that there are no hidden agendas. A management employee who may lose their job may not be pure of heart in a negotiation. An attorney whose motivation is to generate as much as possible in hourly fees may drag out negotiations to the point that a perfectly workable deal falls apart due to frustration and ill will. Of course, the attorney will receive their hourly fees whether the deal works out or not.

You are the buyer or seller. You must make the decision who will negotiate on your behalf. If you are not comfortable being in the middle of it, or if it is your well-developed decision to keep your distance for strategic reasons, make sure that those representing you have your best interests – not theirs – in mind and at heart.

If you can't get to that comfort level with your representative, don't be afraid to negotiate yourself. It is your money and your future – who is going to be your best advocate?

Nevertheless, even if you decide to handle your own negotiations you will need an attorney to be involved. While our last case highlighted some of the downsides of using the wrong attorneys, it should not overshadow the fact that the right attorney is invaluable in the whole process. Attorneys are especially useful in identifying potential personal liabilities in the deal and helping buyers be sure of the transferability of assets. He or she will make sure the lease is transferable and that the proper permits and licenses are in place.

Some who have found a comfort level with their attorney will allow him or her to handle the negotiations. The right attorney may be more likely to be objective, and thus able to avoid the emotions involved in buying or selling a business. They know the legal bumps waiting to trip up buyers and sellers. They know what to reveal and what to keep private. Whether your lawyer handles the negotiations or not, you will need one to assist in identifying problem areas and drafting sales documents. Remember what happened to Gordon in Case No. Seven when he tried to cut corners?

Likewise, don't forget your accountant in the negotiating process. He or she can alert you to methods you can use to make the deal more palatable and advise you about how each method might affect you. Sometimes a change in terms can be more important than a change in price. For example, if a purchase price of $200,000, paid over 10 years at 10% interest is rejected, your accountant may assist you to see that $200,000 over eight years at eight percent interest is what will do the trick. If the new offer is accepted, your accountant has saved you money.

As discussed in our previous case, in some situations both sides will want the other to make the opening bid. The seller is hoping the buyer offers more than he or she hoped, and the buyer is hoping the seller opens with a lower asking price than he or she hoped. Both pad their numbers to leave room for negotiation. Generally, it is the seller who opens with an asking price. In some cases, setting a sale price early on is a good strategy for the seller. It not only provides a starting point from which negotiations may commence but also serves to screen out the looky-loos ready to waste everyone's time.

Buyers should never let on how much they want a business. Sellers should never let on how desperate they are to get rid of a business. There is no place for emotions in negotiations. This game is played with a poker face. Don't make any commitments until consulting with your team of experts. It is perfectly fine, and an excellent strategy, for you to tell the opposing representative that you have to run the terms by your accountant, attorney and/or board of directors.

It is best if negotiations are conducted confidentially. As we have discussed, it benefits neither buyer nor seller to let it leak out that the company is up for sale. As long as no employees are on the premises, negotiating after hours at the business site retains secrecy, while allowing the buyer access to the company's books, ledgers, contracts and other documents, as well as letting the seller demonstrate any operations or procedures involved in the business.

Negotiations generally involve two key components: price and terms of sale. In the complex realm of buying and selling businesses, one is not more important than the other. So don't go in with your focus only on the numbers. Know that terms can swing a deal just as surely as price can.

Negotiations are a complex process of offer and counteroffer. The American way tends toward meeting in the middle. I offer 10, you offer 5, we settle for 7.50. But by using incremental negotiating, you can get yourself a better deal. Let's take this from the point of view of the buyer. The seller asks for $100,000. You think the business is worth around $65,000. You offer $50,000. Meeting you in the middle, the seller asks for $75,000. That's a pretty big step. He or she likely expects you to also meet him or her in the middle with an offer of $62,500. But keep your increments small, sliding the seller down to your level. Tell the seller you really meant $50,000, but maybe you can do $55,000. Explain why you are keeping your offer low or just continue to say you can't do it. As a buyer or a seller, be prepared to walk away if the negotiations aren't progressing to your satisfaction. You can always start up again tomorrow.

If negotiations really bog down it may be a sign that the buyer or seller is not as interested as he or she seemed or he or she is not the decision-maker for the transaction. Also, the buyer's due diligence may have uncovered negative aspects of the business. Or perhaps buyer or seller conditions have changed over the sometimes long time period that has passed up to this point. Accept it as a fact that not every deal closes, but don't give up just yet.

As a buyer, you may want to change your terms in order to bring the seller down on price. Some terms that may be appealing to a seller include:

- structuring the deal so that the seller pays capital gains rather than ordinary income tax (but beware of hidden liabilities)
- structure an installment sale
- structure the deal so that the purchase price goes primarily toward fixed assets
- offer the seller a consulting agreement
- offer to pay more, but over time

If a seller wants to get completely out of the business and never even wants to think about it again, he or she will likely negotiate for an all-cash sale. This should mean a lower price for the buyer. But an all-cash sale doesn't get the seller out from under any personally guaranteed debts he or she has entered into for the company's benefit. If a seller really wants out, he or she will need to get both the buyer's and the lender's permission to transfer his or her personal guarantees to the seller. If the buyer's credit isn't as good as the seller's, the lender won't likely accept that proposal (and most banks will require both buyer and seller personal guarantees without letting anyone off the hook.) As an alternative, the seller can structure the purchase agreement so that those personally guaranteed loans are paid at closing. The seller may even have the check issued to the lender at the closing and wait for a return of the promissory note marked "paid" before the closing is finalized. This protects against the buyer defaulting on the note and the seller becoming responsible on the guarantee.

Representations and Warranties

Representations and warranties are promises of truthfulness put into contractual form in the purchase agreement. During negotiations, sellers say things and buyers say things, and everyone has their spin. But the representations and warranties give the real nitty-gritty. They attest to the truth and accuracy of given information and form one of the most important sections in the purchase agreement. If either side goes against the representations, that party will have breached the agreement.

Because representations and warranties are so important later, they should be dealt with by you now, during the negotiations. Most of the representations will come from the seller. The buyer typically only represents and warrants his or her financial ability to buy the company through the existence of a new corporation formed to acquire the assets and that corporation's authority to carry out the transaction as detailed in the purchase agreement. If the seller is providing financing, the buyer will be asked to represent and warrant the financial condition of the new corporation and its ability to pay the seller. If the seller is not providing financing, he or she will want the buyer to offer up a personal representation and warranty that the buyer has the ability to buy.

The seller, however, is expected to represent and warrant a whole host of terms. He or she may ask that the warranty be limited to a specific range of values.

The following are some of the most important representations made by sellers:

- the seller owns a validly existing corporation (or other entity) that is in good standing and that he or she has the authority to enter into the purchase agreement

- if applicable, the board of directors and/or shareholders approve of the seller entering into the agreement

- the seller owns the assets and such assets will be without liens or encumbrances at the time of closing

- the lease will be in full effect at the time of closing

- all tangible assets will be in good working order at closing

- the seller has no interest in other companies that conduct part of the business

- the seller has no business dealings or interest in any customers' or suppliers' companies that aren't at arm's length

- financial statements have been prepared using consistently applied generally accepted accounting principals, are complete, accurate and fairly represent the financial condition of the seller for the stated periods

- all taxes have been paid in full

- there are no claims, legal proceedings or judgments against the seller, its officers, directors, employees or assets

- no laws, ordinances or regulations applicable to the business have been violated by the seller

- a complete and accurate list of contracts binding the seller have been disclosed through an attached schedule

- the seller will conduct business in the ordinary course; use its best efforts to maintain good relations with customers, employees and suppliers; and take no action that would be adverse to the buyer's interest between the time of signing the agreement and the closing.

- the buyer and his or her representatives will be given full access to the seller's employees, books, records and contracts.

- the seller and his or her accountant will cooperate with the buyer and supply reasonable information prior to closing

Other representations and warranties may be added by the buyer, given the type of business and assets being transferred. Think about what is important to you in the transaction and during negotiations ask that the buyer or seller agree to put a representation and warranty on that point into the purchase agreement.

Letter of Intent

As soon as buyer and seller have come to an agreement on price and major terms, a letter of intent may be prepared. This document precedes the more formal and detailed purchase agreement. It clearly states what each party has agreed to and states that this is all contingent upon the signing of the purchase agreement. It should include price, terms and access buyers will have to sellers' business premises, records, employees, customers and suppliers. A sample Letter of Intent for the Sale of Corporate Assets is provided in Appendix C. Be sure to consult with your professional advisors before drafting and using such an agreement.

Some buyers or sellers may not be 100% certain of the deal at the time of signing the letter of intent. They may request that conditional language be included such as: "This Letter of Intent shall be non-binding until a more formal purchase agreement is signed." Be careful. Just because you have conditional language inserted, doesn't mean that a contract hasn't been formed. If the buyer, for example, in good faith takes all of the steps required under the letter of intent, you as the seller may be precluded from deciding at the last minute not to sign the purchase agreement. There are plenty of court cases where "non-binding" letters of intent have been enforced. The point is, if you go through the negotiation phase and reach an agreement, assume that you are buying or selling the business when you sign the letter of intent. If you are not completely sure about the whole deal, then don't sign the letter of intent. Don't create the legal liability for yourself to buy or sell if that's not what you want to do. It is not fair to you and is certainly not fair to the other person across the table who has likely spent thousands of dollars in attorney, accountant and due diligence fees to get the negotiations to a letter of intent threshold.

That said, there are numerous contingencies that can be placed in a letter of intent (or a purchase agreement) that will protect the buyer. These conditions or precedents to a purchase include the following:

1. Review of the seller's books and records to the buyer's satisfaction.
2. Lining up suitable financing to the buyer's satisfaction.
3. Reviewing and acceptance by the buyer of all lease and purchase agreements.
4. The ability to obtain necessary insurance to the buyer's satisfaction.
5. The occurrence of no material adverse change in the seller's business.

As a general rule, the time period for a review of the books and records will be a fixed and limited time, i.e., 15 or 30 days. If you as buyer are not satisfied after your due diligence investigation you may want to send formal written notice within the time period to the seller of your intent to cancel the sale. You may want your attorney's assistance in preparing this notice letter. Depending on the terms of the agreement, the cancellation letter may perhaps generally read as follows: "Based upon my review of your books and records and pursuant to the 30-day contingency for such review, I have decided not to purchase the business and thus withdraw my offer to purchase dated ...." Such a letter will protect a buyer from a desperate seller willing to use any argument to force a sale.

Rich Dad's Tips

- Negotiations are a crucial stage in buying and selling a business. Be very certain if you are not involved in the process that the person negotiating on your behalf has your best interests at heart.

- Know that terms are just as important as price. The creative use of terms can overcome any objection as to price.

- In the chess game of buying and selling a business, representations and warranties should be considered three moves before you need them. Start locking the other side into statements of truthfulness prior to their inclusion in the purchase agreement.

With the parties agreeing to buy and sell, now it is time to think about ...

Chapter Eleven

Structure

Like anything else that is built to last, your business must have a solid structure. And when buying or selling a business the transaction must have a structure to it as well. A big part of negotiations will be about how to structure the deal. Tax implications, legal considerations and personal preferences will all come into play. Some experts suggest buyer and seller know what structure they want before discussions even begin in order to ease the negotiations. Others think it is the team of experts who should worry about structure after a price has been agreed upon because it may be easier to deal with the subjects of price and structure separately. But price is often affected by structure.

The most basic types of purchase agreement structures are through stock transfer or asset purchase (or a combination of the two). Buyers usually prefer asset purchases, while buyers prefer stock transfers. This subject may cause some of the most heated discussions of the whole process. But compromise is possible. A buyer may take only the assets and pay more or take the stock and pay less. But as we will see in our next case, there are risks to consider.

Asset Purchase

One way to buy and sell a business is through a transfer of assets and cash. Short of an arrangement as a replacement for cash, there is no stock involved. The buyer purchases assets such as equipment, property, customer lists, proprietary information, intellectual property, contracts and agreements. These assets are negotiated for on an asset-by-asset basis and bought at fair market value rather than depreciated book value. Titles must be changed over and filed with the county, and shareholders and directors must approve the sale. Obviously there are tax implications, which are covered in Chapter 13. However, the plus side is that by buying assets rather than stock, the buyer assumes no liabilities other than those, if any, spelled out in the purchase agreement. The company that sold the assets remains a solvent, self-sustaining, legal entity. As such, it is responsible for its own bills. The only liabilities the buyer takes on are the ones the buyer agrees to take on.

Under the Bulk Sales Act (which used to exist in nearly every state but is now in retreat as a requirement), a seller provides a list of the business' creditors and the amount of each debt. The buyer then sends a notice of the impending sale to each creditor, alerting him or her of the asset transfer and stating that, as buyer, he or she will be paying debts as they come due (or at the close, depending on the state's law). Any debts not listed by the seller are the seller's responsibility.

The act is designed to protect creditors, but properly used it will also protect the buyer. If buyer and seller decide to ignore the law, the sale can still go through. However, the seller's creditors can now go against the buyer to collect. Therefore, some sellers will try to convince buyers to skip the hassle of complying with the act. Sellers may even offer indemnification as a substitute. But buyer beware: Even with an indemnification, if the seller doesn't have the cash, creditors will then go after you.

In cases where the business is a non-corporation (such as a sole proprietorship or partnership), an asset purchase is the only option since there is no stock. But a buyer can still purchase the entire company, by declaring the company a single asset to be sold at a single price.

Stock Purchase

Buying stock in a company means becoming an owner of that company. By purchasing all the stock, the buyer becomes the owner of the company and thus controls all of the assets of the company, along with all attendant liens and liabilities. The key here is that the new owner takes on all assets and all liabilities, whether the buyer knows about them or not. The seller may have neglected to tell the buyer about certain aspects of the business (such as lawsuits or IRS actions). To guard against this, the buyer may get an indemnification clause written into the purchase agreement. The clause doesn't prevent the seller from withholding information, nor does it protect the buyer from being sued; it only means that the buyer can sue the seller for any money he or she has to pay to others over contingent (hidden) liabilities. At a later date will the seller be able to cover any claims for damages? You need to ask yourself that. The indemnification clause can be strengthened by structuring the sale so that if the buyer has to pay on contingent liabilities, he or she can withhold that amount from what is still left on any promissory note due the seller.

But as a seller in a stock purchase scenario you must worry that the buyer may come after you from a different front.

Case No. 11 – Don and Beth

Don owned a gravel pit and processing plant in Oregon, and decided it was time to sell. The mill had been in the family for three generations and it was a good, if cyclical, business. He had his business brokers present the opportunity to purchasers across the country. Just as Don was getting nibbles of interest, the processing plant burned down.

It was a difficult time for Don but he persevered. His insurance covered the rebuilding of the plant. He assured potential purchasers that the gravel pit and processing plant would be just as profitable as before.

Beth was an investor out of Ohio. She knew that businesses of the extractive type could be quite lucrative. So she and her attorney flew out to Oregon to consider the business opportunity. They inspected the books and the facility and conducted their due diligence review. Don assured them that the plant would be rebuilt in top operating order. He said that since he hadn't increased the selling price, they were getting a brand new plant for the price of a twenty year-old one.

Beth and her attorney were sufficiently impressed with the deal. As negotiations commenced, Don was quite insistent that he wanted to structure the transaction as a stock sale instead of an asset purchase. He had held the stock for many years and it was much better tax planning for he and his family to simply sell the shares of the existing company to Beth.

Beth and her attorney were hesitant at first. What if there were any unknown or undisclosed liabilities against the company? Don assured them that there weren't any, and just to allay their fears, offered to fully indemnify them and leave $300,000 in an escrow account for one year to satisfy any unknown claims. He also agreed to significantly reduce the purchase price if they would accept a stock purchase.

The numbers at the price Don was offering make sense to Beth. It was agreed that she would take over the business once the new plant was finished. A deal for the purchase of shares was concluded. But almost immediately after taking over, things went sour for Beth in the business. The construction company was feuding with the engineering company over the plant, because neither of them could get it to process the gravel properly. She was paying out huge monthly expenses and generating no real revenue. Losses were mounting and none of Don's projections that Beth had relied upon were even close to being met.

Beth was furious. She instructed her attorney to look into a lawsuit against Don. The attorney reported back that under the securities laws, a very strong case could be made. He informed Beth that both federal and state securities laws contained strict anti-fraud provisions to deal with any misrepresentations or material omissions of fact in the sale of stock. If Beth relied on an untrue statement or a material fact was omitted that she would have relied upon in making a decision to purchase the company, a securities fraud claim could be brought. Originally, these provisions were to protect against improper stock sales to widows, orphans and uninformed passive purchasers. But in 1985, the United States Supreme

Court ruled that anti-fraud provisions applied to private transactions involving the sale of one hundred percent of the shares to a purchaser of the business.

Beth's attorney informed her that because the stock had been sold under this new definition, Don could be sued for alleged misrepresentations in the sale of the business. If Beth had instead purchased the assets of the business, they would not have been able to bring such a powerful suit. This, he explained, was due to the strong public policy in favor of protecting purchasers of stock.

Beth sued under the anti-fraud provisions of the securities laws. Don was wiped out.

It is important to recognize that there are significant risks for both buyers and sellers in a stock purchase transaction. The buyer, as we saw in Gordon's case, may be acquiring unknown and ruinous liabilities. The seller, as in Don's case, may be held to an incredibly high standard of candor and disclosure under the securities laws. Some lawyers will make the case that with proper and detailed representations in the purchase agreement, a securities law fraud claim may be contractually eliminated or minimized. But the field of securities law is extremely complex and subject to shifting definitions and inconsistent rulings from court to court. Because of the uncertainty, not many angels like to tread this ground. Both buyers and sellers must be careful when considering a stock purchase transaction.

If a seller absolutely must engage in a stock purchase transaction, and a promissory note is involved, the seller should retain a security interest in the stock to ensure the buyer does not resell the business without his or her permission. The seller will want the right to qualify potential new buyers to be sure his or her original note gets paid. If the stock is secured, the buyer does not get the stock certificates even after the closing. In fact, the buyer will not get the certificates and full ownership of stock until all notes are paid.

This still may not be enough to guarantee your security. In order to stop the buyer from creating or issuing new stock, making the seller's now-diluted security less valued or worthless, the seller needs to get an anti-dilution provision written into the purchase agreement.

A dilution example helps to explain. Suppose in a stock transaction, Seller, Inc. gives up 100% of its shares in exchange for 10% of the shares in Buyer, Inc. Seller, Inc. now owns 1 million shares, or 10% of the 10 million shares issued by Buyer, Inc. But Buyer, Inc. has 30 million more unissued shares in reserve, and it starts issuing them to its officers, directors, consultants - everyone but Seller, Inc. As a result, Seller, Inc.'s ownership interest is being diluted. Whereas with 10 million shares issued it owned 10% of Buyer, Inc., with 40 million shares now issued, Seller, Inc.'s ownership of 1 million shares is diluted down to only a 2.5% interest in Buyer, Inc. You can be certain that this happens with regularity. To prevent it, anti-dilution provisions allowing Buyer, Inc. to maintain its 10% interest in Seller, Inc. for a certain period of time no matter how many shares Seller, Inc. cares to issue should be considered.

The seller may also want to retain security interest in the company's assets (including accounts receivable) to prevent the buyer from reducing the company to a shell, thus making the stock worthless. More than one buyer has bought a company with the intent of looting it and disappearing. As always, make sure you know who you are doing business with and then, even if they do pass muster, protect yourself as if you didn't trust them in the first place.

Merger

A merger involves certain stock-related transactions when the company is a corporation. Although technically not the purchase or sale of a business, mergers are frequently used to accomplish certain financial or liquidity goals of a company. Though there are a variety of kinds of mergers, the most common are forward and reverse. A forward merger is one where the acquired company is merged into the buyer's company and disappears.

FORWARD MERGER

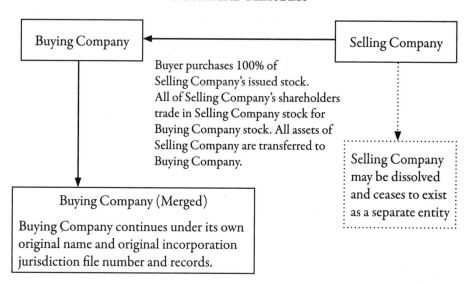

Buying Company

Buyer purchases 100% of Selling Company's issued stock. All of Selling Company's shareholders trade in Selling Company stock for Buying Company stock. All assets of Selling Company are transferred to Buying Company.

Selling Company

Buying Company (Merged)

Buying Company continues under its own original name and original incorporation jurisdiction file number and records.

Selling Company may be dissolved and ceases to exist as a separate entity

REVERSE MERGER

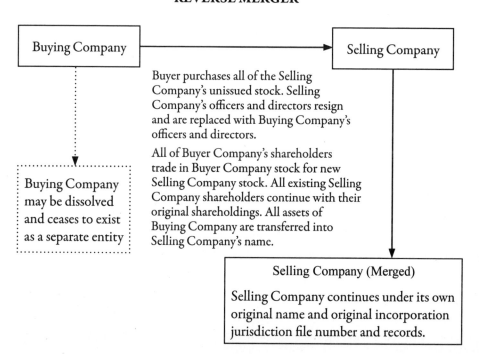

Buying Company

Buyer purchases all of the Selling Company's unissued stock. Selling Company's officers and directors resign and are replaced with Buying Company's officers and directors.

All of Buyer Company's shareholders trade in Buyer Company stock for new Selling Company stock. All existing Selling Company shareholders continue with their original shareholdings. All assets of Buying Company are transferred into Selling Company's name.

Selling Company

Buying Company may be dissolved and ceases to exist as a separate entity

Selling Company (Merged)

Selling Company continues under its own original name and original incorporation jurisdiction file number and records.

A reverse merger is simply the opposite, where the buyer's company is merged into the seller's, with only the acquired company remaining. The buyer usually purchases all or most of the stock belonging to the seller's officers, directors and controlling shareholders, and transfers that stock into the names of its own officers and directors. That effectively transfers control of the selling company over to the buyer, and allows the buyer to move forward as the selling company. With control of the selling company, the buyer can then integrate its existing business into the seller, leaving the buyer's corporate existence behind. The purchase price can be paid with cash, stock in another company or a combination. This plan may work well with a target company with a good reputation. Of course, the seller and its officers, directors and controlling shareholders will want to be compensated for that reputation.

It must be noted that a reverse merger can be disastrous for a clean company merging into a selling company with problems. If you must take this route, be certain to do your highest level due diligence on any such candidate and include a multitude of representations and warranties that may get you out of the deal if needed. Be sure to work with an experienced attorney and accountant as well, because in the world of reverse mergers there is an ongoing litany of unclean shell companies being used to promote fraud, abuse and staggering losses for innocent shareholders.

Covenants Not to Compete/Goodwill

As a buyer, you probably don't want the seller to open another company in the same industry, compete with you in the same town or later consult for a company that is or will become a rival. If you don't want the seller to compete with you once the sale is final, you need to get such a prohibition in writing. You can have either a separate non-compete agreement or include a limiting provision in the purchase agreement. The agreement should also prohibit disclosing trade secrets and proprietary information. Such agreements are complicated and must stand up in court if enforcement is ever needed. Drafting these documents is definitely a job for your attorney.

In doing so it is important to understand that our public policy, those big picture goals for courts and legislatures to chew on, is to encourage people to work. A contract that prevents someone from working for too long a time period in too broad of a scope will not be upheld by a court. Although each state has its own rules, as a general rule, an agreement that prevents someone from working for longer than three or four years is usually not upheld by most courts. Also know that in California covenants not to compete are void as against public policy, except in very narrow cases, which can include the sale of a business. As well, in Virginia, covenants not to compete are enforced only in very limited cases. Be sure to work with a local attorney when entering into this arena.

A well-drafted agreement not to compete (or a consulting agreement that keeps the seller on board for a period of time) can save the buyer on taxes. In an asset sale, when the purchase price is spread over assets, the seller will pay taxes on any gain, no matter how the price is allocated. In a stock purchase, the tax effect for the seller is likewise no different. But for the buyer, how the purchase price is allocated is certainly an issue. If the buyer can allocate part of the price to an agreement not to compete with that payment to be paid over the term of non-competition, an advantage can be had. The buyer can amortize that part of the purchase price attributable to the non-compete, giving him or her a much faster write-off than that which would come from the slower write-offs associated with land, goodwill or other assets.

The IRS will amortize the value allocated to the non-compete agreement over a 15 year period. The income is taxed to the recipient when received. There are tax planning opportunities to allocate a lower amount to the covenant, and a higher amount to the other depreciable or amortizable assets. As well, if it is an asset sale, the buyer and seller may have different motivations on the allocation of the purchase price due to ordinary income recapture on depreciated personal property. So be sure to work with your CPA on how the income is characterized. Arm's length negotiations usually are upheld by the IRS.

Rich Dad's Tips

- Unless there is a thoroughly overwhelming reason to engage in a stock purchase transaction, consider entering into an asset purchase agreement.

- Be extremely careful: A significant number of reverse merger transactions do not work out well for the good guys.

- When drafting a covenant not to compete be sure to consult with your attorney as to local court standards and acceptable time and geographic constraints.

An integral part of the negotiation process will be how the deal will be financed ...

Chapter Twelve

Financial Strategies

Case No. 12 – Jim and Lisa

Lisa owned an educational products company that sold parent/teacher aids, children's books and an exclusive line of instructional board games. In seven years, she had built the company up from her kitchen table to the point that it was now grossing over $20 million a year in sales. Lisa owned 100% of the S corporation's stock and received fairly significant flow-through profits each year. But the business required all of her time, and she was ready to spend more time with her husband and family.

Jim owned Z-Ed, Inc., a company that marketed educational products directly to school districts. Lisa's company was a perfect fit for Jim for it allowed Z-Ed, Inc. to offer Lisa's exclusive line of products to the schools and gave him new distribution channels that had been developed by Lisa for Jim's existing products.

An asset purchase agreement was reached, whereby Z-Ed, Inc. paid Lisa $3 million in cash and gave her a promissory note for $4 million to be paid over five years. Lisa wanted the promissory note to be secured by the asset she was transferring. Jim was agreeable, but said that such security would have to be subordinated (put below, in second place) to the security given to the bank that was loaning Z-Ed, Inc. the $3 million for Lisa's down payment.

Lisa was not pleased by this information. Jim was using all debt (the bank's $3 million loan and the $4 million note to Lisa) to acquire the business. The fact that none of Jim's own money or Z-Ed Inc.'s own money was being used was of concern. At the same time, Lisa was now more and more ready to get out of the business. Three million dollars in her pocket would be a nice payday.

Still, she needed to protect herself as best she could. Four million dollars was a lot to lose if things went bad and the promissory note was not honored and paid. Interestingly, she noticed that the bank was only seeking a security interest in Lisa's assets that amounted to all inventory, equipment, accounts receivable and customer files and information. The bank was not, at this point, seeking security in Lisa's intellectual property – the trademarks, copyrights and other proprietary rights associated with the instructional board games. Lisa knew that these were the most valuable assets she had.

Lisa and her lawyer promptly arranged for her $4 million promissory note to be secured by the intellectual property being transferred to Jim's company. Lisa felt much better about her position in the deal by having such security.

The transaction closed and Lisa received her $3 million payment. Seven years of hard work had paid off for her. Now she could live comfortably and perhaps even more comfortably if she could collect on Z-Ed, Inc.'s $4 million promissory note to her over the next five years.

That was not to be. Shortly thereafter, Z-Ed, Inc. was charged with bribing school district purchasing agents to purchase Z-Ed, Inc. products. A sting operation caught two Z-Ed, Inc. sales representatives on video tape offering cash and female favors in exchange for volume purchases. The immediate and widespread negative publicity ruined Z-Ed, Inc., overnight. It never made another sale to a school district, or anyone else, for that matter.

Obviously, Z-Ed, Inc. defaulted on the promissory note to Lisa. She and her lawyer promptly took steps to have the intellectual property returned to her. After several minor skirmishes in bankruptcy court, Lisa was back in control of her intellectual property.

As happens to a not-insignificant percentage of those who take a note in the sale of a business, Lisa was now back running the business she had just sold. It was not her plan, but she now held valuable assets and couldn't very well let them sit idle. Although not in this case, many times there are continuing obligations which had been personally guaranteed by the seller prior to the sale, thus forcing the seller to step in and run the business just to at least make the payments.

Lisa had taken the risk that the promissory note would not be paid. She could have negotiated a purchase price of $5 million all in cash with no promissory note. She and her lawyer had gone through such a strategy. But for her, $3 million in cash with the chance at another $4 million more was a more attractive offer. She knew the chances when she entered into the deal.

Now she had her valuable line of instructional board games back. So, she set about marketing them all over again, building up the business and hopefully selling to the right company in the future.

Lisa's case illustrates what can happen when a seller takes a promissory note in the sale of a business. In her situation, Lisa did not fare too badly. After all, she was able to keep the $3 million down payment and received a return of her assets in a way that allowed her to continue sales. Many sellers aren't so fortunate. Frequently they will be forced to come back into a business that has been gutted, if not totally destroyed, by mismanagement and negative goodwill. To come back in and try to turn around such a wreckage can be a Herculean task. A seller needs to be careful, and factor in the possibility of a return to the business, when taking a promissory note.

A buyer, on the other hand, who does not have the purchase price in hand, will have to decide whether to borrow the money from a bank or from the seller, or both. In each case, interest payments need to be considered in the purchase price. And if the loan comes from a bank, loan origination fees, points and other charges will need to be added in. Also, if the loan comes in the form of a carry from the seller, the buyer will likely be looking at a higher purchase price and higher interest costs.

Loans

Businesses need money. Startup money, working capital, acquisition financing. There's no business that works without it. Loans are a typical way to satisfy such needs.

Two categories of loans are common for the transfer of a business: acquisition loans and working capital loans. Acquisition loans run for five to twenty years or longer. Working capital loans usually run for one to three years and are renewed or renegotiated at maturity. When buying a business, buyers sometimes forget about working capital. Don't. It's like forgetting life blood. You can't survive without it.

Odds are the purchase deal involves some cash. Odds are the buyer doesn't have it tucked beneath the mattress in the spare room. So loans are a reality of the process. But be consoled by the fact that is easier to get a loan for an existing business than for a startup venture due to the business' track record, assets and its ability to attract other financing (such as a carrying loan by the seller).

Buyers should research banks in the same way they research everything else. Banks specialize. Some shy away from all business loans, some radiate toward only large business loans. Look for a bank that is friendly to your situation, familiar with your type of loan and willing to continue a relationship with you after the close. Banks need to make loans to stay in business. Under the right circumstances, they will compete for your business. Let them. While interest rates are likely the same from bank to bank, security interests, points, origination fees and other charges may vary widely. Shop around, and don't be afraid to negotiate your terms.

Before you face the loan committee, have your paperwork in order. Most banks will want to see business financial statements, personal financial statements and tax returns, corporate charters and other organizational documents, and a business plan. Any other documents you can provide (such as a list of equipment and real estate, a table of the age of accounts receivable and payable, and your resume) will help convince the committee of your ability to run a successful enterprise.

If you apply for a loan at a bank where you are already a good customer, ask about the bank's preferred rate. Most banks have a prime and preferred rate. Getting the preferred rate may shave up to a quarter of one percent off the interest rate. To get the preferred rate, offer to do all of your personal and business banking there to help make your case. Another perk you can negotiate for from your bank is a suspension of principal payments or a reduced interest rate for six months to a year (or more if you can swing it).

You may want to consider programs offered by the Small Business Administration (SBA). Their many programs, which include the very popular and useful Service Corps of Retired Executives (SCORE) program and other business advice services have successfully helped millions of entrepreneurs and business owners. Likewise, their loan programs have helped launch many worthy businesses. While the SBA no longer directly makes loans, it can still help you by guaranteeing a loan from a bank. The SBA offers the banks a safety net by promising to pay back the loan if you default. If this happens, the SBA will then come after you for the money. The SBA will usually only guarantee up to 90 percent of the loan, so banks will still want to be sure you are a good risk of their money. Besides, if you are a risk a bank is unlikely to take, the same is probably true for the SBA. They will certainly want to see the same documents you would prepare for a loan committee to assist in their decision making.

SBA-guaranteed loans offer several advantages over a loan you might get on your own. First off, you are more attractive to banks with that guarantee behind you. Although not always, in some cases it may be easier to negotiate terms (such as a longer payback rate). Also, since the SBA puts a ceiling on interest rates a bank can charge, you'll save points.

Start with the banker. He or she will direct you to the SBA at the appropriate point in the process. If the bank doesn't deal with the SBA, consider seeking out different banks.

Seller Takes Note or Stock

As we saw in our last case, as a seller, you will likely not get the entire purchase price in cash. Therefore, how the business is run after the closing is still important to you. If the business doesn't do well, you may find yourself stuck with a useless note or stock, or back running the company you wanted to be free from.

A good broker will qualify the buyer, making sure he or she has the ability to finance the deal. If you are not using a broker, you should be doing this yourself (with the help of your team). Don't be shy about nosing into the buyer's finances. Don't just look at the purchase price, either. You will need to be sure the buyer has enough capital to make it through bad patches, especially the tough transitional one that tends to follow on the heels of a purchase.

Most sales involve some sort of carry by the seller. Buyers should be somewhat cautious of sellers who want all the money up front. Do they have something to hide? Are they totally behind the sale? Or, as in our last case, were they burned in a prior sale? If so, what happened? You should know the history.

If the seller does offer a carry, he or she will likely require the buyer to provide security for the payment of the promissory note. If possible, buyers should not grant blanket security. If he or she grants a security interest in all assets, it is unlikely that a bank will be willing to lend money for expansions or improvements. However, the seller may be willing to subordinate his or her security interest. It's worth checking. And note that while in one section we've said the note-carrying seller should get maximum protection on all assets and here we're saying the buyer should not allow the seller to have all assets secured, the polarity reflects the dynamics of a negotiated transaction. The buyer and seller must negotiate what is important to them. Where things end up will be different in every deal.

Buyers should beware of notes calling for balloon payments (where a large sum is due at the end of a certain term) being made in less than five years. The reality of running the business may not meet your expectations and leave you hanging for a sum you can't possibly pay or even finance.

The seller may accept contingency payments. This involves setting goals for the business. The buyer will pay a certain amount at closing and an additional amount later, but only if the business meets certain sales targets. This can be a good deal, given buyer and seller are comfortable with each other's skills and prospects. When the seller has a stake in the profits, he or she is likely to want to be part of management or at least helpful towards management.

A seller may opt to take stock in the buyer's company as part of the purchase payment. Relative valuation of both buyer and seller stock should be considered in determining the number of shares to be transferred.

A seller may also take convertible securities as payment. In this way, the seller offers the buyer a note or loan that, at the end of the loan's life, may be converted to company stock. The benefit to the seller is that he or she has the opportunity of owning stock – with hopefully a future upside potential – in the company, while still having an income source for the years during the loan life. The benefit to the buyer is that he or she does not dilute stock at the time of purchase and perhaps later does not pay a portion of the loan back due to a conversion to stock by the seller.

Personal Guarantees

In general, it is easier to get a loan for a manufacturing or distribution business – businesses with fixed assets that a bank can reach in the event of a default. Without such fixed assets, you will likely have to offer up a pledge of your own personal assets as security. If so, negotiate a deal where assets are released (or become free from security restrictions) as part of the debt is paid and try to keep your personal residence out of the mix. But for all your negotiating skills you may find that a personal guarantee is an absolute requirement to seal the deal. You're taking a risk. Hopefully, you've thought it all through. You've discussed it over with your family and circle of advisors. If it is the right move, you will sign the guarantee and become personally responsible for the success or failure of your business.

Rich Dad's Tips

- Taking a promissory note back as a seller involves risk. Be very comfortable with the buyer, as well as their skill, experience and ethics, when accepting such a payment plan.

- Banks are willing to compete for you business so be sure to shop around. Also, through lead groups or chamber mixers consider getting to know one or more community bankers in your area. Such professional relationships can help pave the way for future beneficial borrowings.

- Again, creative terms can often lead to win/win scenarios. Be open to solutions that provide for mutual benefit.

And now it is time to discuss everyone's favorite issue: taxes.

Chapter Thirteen

Taxation

Case No. 13: – Fritz and Mona

Fritz and Mona owned a profitable golf shop. Fritz had been on the PGA Tour, had been a local pro in the area and knew everyone in town. Mona was equally as well known, and knew how to run a business. Together they ran a strong golf headquarters outlet.

But Fritz knew it was time to retire. The larger box stores were moving in and his younger clientel cared more about prices than advice and service. (He had warned the PGA that without a proper foundation the next generation of golfers would not stick with the game. As his warnings had nothing to do with corporate sponsorships, they were ignored.) Fritz and Mona were also looking forward to a good retirement and that was their official reason for selling the business.

Mona and Fritz met with Tom, their CPA, to discuss the business sale. The first question they had was how much money they would have to pay in taxes. Like any good professional, Tom said: "It depends." Tom further explained that when you are planning for taxes on a business sale there are five factors to consider:

    (1)   What You are Selling
    (2)   How You are Selling
    (3)   Business Structure
    (4)   Length of Ownership
    (5)   When and How You Will Be Paid

Two Ways to Sell

The first step is to determine exactly what you are selling.

Mona was confused. They were selling the golf store. That was correct, Tom explained, but there are two way to do it:

(1)   You can sell the assets of the business; or

(2)   You can sell the ownership of the business.

In the first scenario, if you operate as a corporation of LLC, you can sell the corporate shares or membership interests so that the new buyer takes over the entity. Or, in the second scenario, you can sell the assets of the business – equipment, inventory, customer lists and the like – the the buyer. Let's understand how an asset sale works.

Selling the Assets

The assets of a business are generally comprised of many things – inventory, furniture, fixed assets and certain intellectual property, including patents, trademarks and copyrights. The IRS requires that both the buyer and seller agree on what is being bought and sold. The tax consequences for both buyer and seller differ depending on the class (as determined by the IRS) used.

The classes that the IRS recognizes are:

(1)   Class I: These are the liquid assets of the business such as cash and general deposit accounts (including savings and checking accounts).

(2)   Class II: These are assets which are actively traded personal property such as certificates of deposit, foreign currency (even if they are not actively traded), U.S. government securities and publicly traded stock.

(3)   Class III: These are assets such as accounts receivable, mortgages, and credit card receivables from customers that arise in the ordinary course of business.

(4)   Class IV: These are items that would normally be considered inventory assets or property that is sold in the ordinary course of business.

(5)   Class V: These are all assets other than Class I, II, III, IV, VI and VII.

(6)   Class VI: These are intangible assets, which means that they are more intellectual – not real or tangible in the physical sense. An example would be intellectual property such as patents, trade secrets and the like. Basically, it includes all intangible assets except those covered in Class VII.

(7)   Class VII: These are the assets of goodwill and going concern value (such as workforce in place and customer (or client) lists.

Both the buyer and seller are required to report the breakdown of the sale to the IRS. And, if the buyer and seller report different breakdowns, the IRS is only too happy to jump in to audit both to determine their own breakdown. This breakdown is called the "allocation."

As an example, Tom suggested that Mona and Fritz negotiate a sale of the assets of their business for $1,000,000. Part of the negotiation might include a breakdown of $10,000 for the cash accounts, $20,000 for the accounts receivable, $50,000 for equipment and $920,000 for the goodwill of the client. The breakdown by class would be:

Class I	$ 10,000
Class III	$ 20,000
Class V	$ 50,000
Class VII	$ 920,000

Both Mona and Fritz and their buyer would report this allocation on their tax returns for the year of the sale.

Tax Consequences for the Seller

Generally, the seller will pay tax based on two different income tax rates – an ordinary income tax rate and a capital gains rate. The capital gains rate is usually lower than the ordinary tax rate.

If the seller has held the assets of the business for over one year, the assets are capital assets. That means a lower tax rate for most taxpayers. However, there is an exception made for property that is used in the trade or business. In this case, the gain related to these items is taxed at the generally higher ordinary income tax rate. Regardless of how long the assets are held, the result is the same for these assets – a higher tax rate.

Examples of property that the IRS states must be excluded from the capital gains rate are inventory, stock in trade, and property held primarily for sale to customers in the ordinary course of the taxpayer's trade or business.

And, the professional's favorite answer, "It depends!" applies when you are determining what is a capital gains item and what is an asset used in the trade or business. That is because each person's circumstances are different. For example, one taxpayer could have a desk as a capital asset if it is something they use in their computer consulting business. But, another taxpayer may have the desk as an inventory item, because that is what they sell in their business.

One item to note – regardless of how long you own personal or real property, if you have previously depreciated the property, you are required to add back in the value of that depreciation at the ordinary tax rate. This "add back" is called recapture. For example, if you have equipment originally purchased for $100,000, which has been depreciated by $20,000, and then eventually sell it for $130,000. You will first have to "recapture" the $20,000 depreciation. The $20,000 is taxed at your ordinary tax rate. You then can take $30,000 of gain at the capital gains rate.

Tax Consequences for the Buyer

The buyer is allowed to allocate the purchase price against the various classes of assets. But, remember the buyer needs to report the same allocation as the seller did. And, this is where negotiation can be so important to the deal.

For example, if the golf shop buyer can allocate a large part of the sales price to the inventory of golf clubs, it increases their costs of goods sold. So if the buyer negotiate an allocation of $30,000 against, 1,000 golf clubs, they have a per club cost of $30 ($30,000 ÷ 1,000). When they later sell a club for $50, they can record a cost of $30 (the average allocable cost) against the income. Their profit is $20. If the club would normally cost $20, the buyer is $10 ahead due to their advantageous allocation since in a normal setting their profit would not be $20 but $30.

For the buyer, it is important to have as much as possible allocated to items that he will quickly expense in the business. Otherwise, if he has to "capitalize" the assets, he carries those items on the balance sheet for a long time, perhaps forever. He has then paid money for something for which he can not get a taxable deduction.

The buyer will likely want to allocate a large amount of the sales price to the inventory. This type of basis allocation is used quickly against income from the business. On the other hand, the basis allocated to intangible property such as client lists and goodwill is amortized over 15 years. This reduces income from the business at a much slower rate. In the case of fixed assets such as equipment, the buyer must depreciate the assets using the standard tables of depreciable lives which range anywhere from five to thirty-nine years. So again, allocation is important.

Stock Sale

Tom then reviewed with Fritz and Mona the advantages of a stock sale. With a stock sale, if the stock has been held over one year, the entire amount received by the sellers would be taxed at capital gains rates. As we have said, these rates are generally much lower than ordinary income rates so there is a definite advantage to the sellers to do a stock sale. (As well, there may be even more generous tax rates or incentives that Congress offers from time to time. So check with your CPA to see if these are currently in effect.)

But it is important to know that there is a real risk to the seller in buying your stock. As discussed in Case No. 8 involving Morgan and Gordon, in buying your stock the seller assumes all of the Company's liabilities. These may include unknown hazardous waste issues, a sexual harassment case or some other out of the blue company killer. In my practice, when representing a buyer and seeking to avoid liability, I always pursue an asset sale instead of a stock sale. But some sellers will accept less money for a stock sale due to their lower tax rates. Each deal is different but what is consistent is that buyers have to be careful in how they buy.

How You Are Selling

Tom next reviewed how Mona and Fritz would be paid. Sometimes buyers offered a down payment and a note to secure payment over time. Sometimes they offered an all cash payment. Fritz said that they were looking at a strictly cash purchase. That meant all of the gain from the sale would be taxable when the sale occurred.

In other cases, a buyer may want to make payments for the purchase over time. This means that the sale is an installment sale. In the case of an installment sale, a note will be drawn. The IRS requires that a fair interest rate be assigned to the note from an installment sale. If there isn't an interest rate for the note, the IRS is only to happy to create (or "impute") one of their own, and then tax the "interest" received as income.

Each payment that the seller receives will be comprised of principal, reducing the note balance from the sale, and interest. The interest is current income for seller and a current expense for the buyer.

The seller also must make a calculation as to gain for the principal portion of the sale. To calculate the amount of gain, the basis (cost) of the assets is subtracted from the total sales price. The result is called the gross profit. The percentage of gross profit is then applied to each payment's principal amount. Sound confusing? It is! Plus, there are other circumstances to be taken into account such as the recapture of depreciation, as discussed earlier. This is one calculation you want to have prepared by a tax expert.

Business Structure

Mona and Fritz's business was in a C corporation structure. A C corporation, unlike an S corporation, had profits taxed at the corporate level. After tax profits distributed to shareholders were then taxed again at the shareholder level. Their C corporation added even more complications to the sale because if the sale was done wrong, they could be forced into liquidating their C corporation. This could potentially lead to "double taxation," as the liquidation would force a liquidating dividend. Luckily, Mona and Fritz had planned for this exit strategy and set up the business so even an asset sale from their golf shop business would not force a liquidation.

If their business had been within an S Corporation or Limited Liability Company (LLC), Mona and Fritz may not have been able to take advantage of the special tax incentives Congress offers from time to time. That said, the sale would have been much easier to orchestrate in one of these structures without the risk of double taxation that comes from a C Corporation.

Length of Ownership

Wherever possible, you will want to take capital gains treatment of the tax on the sale of your business. There are two elements to determining capital gains:

(1) The type of asset
(2) The length of time that you have owned the asset

Work with your CPA to determine the nature of your assets and the corresponding tax treatment. Beware that your amount of profit may be significantly greater with ordinary income tax treatment as opposed to capital gains treatment.

When and How You Will Be Paid

Most businesses are bought with the more standard fare of a combination of cash and a note. However, the following paragraph may come true for you.

Small business makes good and sells out to a Forbes 400 mega-giant! It's not impossible that this could happen to your company. And, suddenly, you are thrust into a much more sophisticated world of tax advantaged mergers and sales. It is possible that you can have tax-deferred stock exchanges that give you assets of another company and delay paying the tax. There are many possibilities and you definitely want an experienced team of tax experts. One thing you can be sure of – the big guys will have their own team!

Selling Smart

Selling smart doesn't mean just price. Understanding the taxation element in the sale of a business can mean selling for a lower price, and taking home more money. Be sure to get your advisors on board early in the process so you can shape the transaction to your advantage. And by appreciating the tax law, you and your team will hopefully keep more of the sales proceeds.

Rich Dad's Tips

- If you are selling the assets of your business, negotiate for increased allocated value to capital gains assets, so you pay less tax.

- If your business is currently in a C Corporation, make sure your corporation doesn't terminate with the sale of the main business. One strategy would be to negotiate a management contract over time between the purchasing company and your C Corporation. In all cases, get good tax advice first!

- Don't forget that the IRS requires a form filed with tax returns for both the buyer and seller for newly sold business. The single biggest argument I see after the sale between the buyer and seller is completely avoidable! Make sure your contract spells out all the details so that the buyer and seller can consistently report the sale on their tax returns. It is in everyone's best interest to avoid an IRS audit.

Now let's review the contract for it all ...

Chapter Fourteen

The Purchase and Sale Agreement

Once all the details of the purchase have been hammered out, the buyer and seller sign a purchase agreement, which is usually prepared by the buyer's lawyer. It all comes down to the purchase agreement. More than goods or services, it is the agreement that is being sold, the agreement that carries the weight of the law. Therefore, it should be as detailed as possible to avoid any misunderstandings at the time of closing or in the future.

Most purchase agreements protect the buyer, with most of the representations and warranties favoring him or her. The main section the seller should pay attention to (not that there is any section the seller should ignore) will be the promissory note. If the buyer defaults on the note, you can sue, but what good does that do if the buyer can't afford to pay? If the buyer declares bankruptcy, the seller may not even be able to bring suit. The security behind the promissory note may be all that is available to the seller if the buyer can't pay. Therefore, sellers need to be very tough during negotiations for security.

Analyzing the Provisions

As with any contractual agreement, there are particular components necessary to make the document legally binding. All contracts must include details of what is covered in the agreement and details as to what each party is giving up in the exchange. Both parties must get something of value. Both parties must give up something of value. If not, the courts will hold that there was a failure of consideration, and unwind the whole transaction. A free lunch is not a good thing in the sale of a business.

If you haven't guessed already, let's get this straight: a purchase agreement is not the place to try your hand at writing. Your attorney should know all the loopholes by which each party can get the largest part of the pie. Buyer: have your attorney prepare the agreement. Seller: have your attorney go over the agreement with you, adding, deleting and changing information where necessary. But keep in mind that attorneys are usually only experts at legal matters. Your business judgment should not be put aside in this stage of the game. Keep your wits about you and don't be afraid to second-guess the experts and make them explain their reasoning.

As with all other documents involved with buying or selling a business, there is no one format to follow. Your lawyer will help you determine the order of sections, which information to include, bury or leave out, and how to title each section. The following is a brief summary of the common sections of an asset purchase agreement:

1. Parties and Locations: Include the companies involved and the primary locations of facilities. The buyer will want to include individual shareholders as owners as well as the company itself in case he or she has to sue the seller over representations and warranties. Many companies dissolve after a sale, and the buyer does not want to be left with no entity to sue.

2. Assets and Liabilities: List all assets and liabilities being transferred by the agreement. If the purchase is of individual assets, include a complete list as an attachment. The seller will want this list included to be sure the buyer understands that not everything used in the business is part of the sale (some assets may not even be owned by the business). The buyer will want to include verbiage stating that the seller owns all assets and that they will be transferred free and clear of any debts, liens or encumbrances. Also include all liabilities and obligations, and state which will be

transferred from seller to buyer. Only assets and liabilities listed will become the responsibility of the buyer.

3. Purchase Price and Allocation: Detail all money matters here. Who pays what, how much and when. Include how the price is allocated among the assets, what percentage is due at signing (usually 5 percent to 10 percent), what percentage at closing (in cash or promissory note) and any other financial arrangements to which the parties have agreed. Details of the financial agreement will be included as an attachment. But don't worry about details of the promissory note in this section. If a note is part of the deal, it most likely will be detailed in a separate supplemental section.

4. Closing: Date, location and any other details of the closing should be included. Keep in mind that the closing date listed is usually a target only. Either buyer or seller (or both) can postpone for a reasonable time (usually 30 days). However, if the closing date needs to be firm, it should be stated in the best legal terms possible. Then, if the seller doesn't turn over the business on that date, the buyer can sue. And if the buyer does not deliver the agreed upon money, the seller can sue. This sort of line in the sand is not recommended, however. After all, life happens even when you're busy with a business deal. People get ill, families have issues and closing dates become unrealistic or even impossible. No one wants to get this far in the process and end up losing a deposit or even the entire deal because of inflexibility in the timeline.

5. Non-Competition and Consulting Agreements: This section will simply reference the existence of such agreements. Supplemental attachments should be included to detail the terms.

6. Representations and Warranties: The truth is out, and it is guaranteed in this section. Both buyers and sellers have made promises and here's where those promises are spelled out along with the consequences of misrepresentations. This section cuts to the heart of the matter (as mentioned in Chapter 10) and can get quite complicated. Have the attorneys spend extra time on it and be sure they understand what

both buyer and seller are promising. This section is most definitely a group effort. Many of those representations and warranties will be cast as surviving the agreement, meaning they will be true at closing and into the future. Be sure to appreciate the consequences of surviving guarantees.

7. Conditions to Closing: Buyer and seller will usually agree to perform certain tasks before the closing. These tasks are detailed here along with remedies and penalties for failure to meet the requirements. This can be a parachute for the buyer, allowing him or her to leave the deal. The buyer will want the conditions to be as broad as possible. At a minimum, the buyer will want to be sure that there will be no adverse material changes (financial or physical) in the business or its assets and that the seller has been granted necessary shareholder or owner consent for the transfer. Reasonable sellers will not object to these minimum points. The buyer is looking for the business to be run just as before in the time between the purchase agreement being signed and the closing. He or she will want the seller to notify him or her of any changes, such as granting pre-arranged raises or bonuses, or signing minor contracts needed in the due course of business. The buyer would not want, for example, the seller to sign on and institute an expensive new ad campaign prior to closing, or to become obligated for any other major transaction.

8. Indemnification: A basic indemnification clause sets forth the seller's agreement to reimburse the buyer for any monetary loss due to a breach by the seller of the representations and warranties. The buyer will likely set aside part of the purchase price (called a holdback) at the closing to take care of any contingent liabilities or debts, but he or she may not set aside enough. Plus, he or she can only set that money aside for a finite period of time. The buyer will want his or her attorney to be named as escrow agent if they are willing to serve in such a role. The seller may want an independent escrow agent. As for the amount of the holdback, buyers usually want larger holdbacks than sellers. The indemnification adds

protection against problems that pop up after the holdback period expires. Buyers should be sure that the amount held back at closing is enough to cover legal fees if they have to sue. Buyers should also make sure the seller's indemnities are signed by the individual shareholders personally, since so many corporations dissolve after assets are sold. This is another one of those sections that can be complicated and cause problems if not thoroughly understood by both buyer and seller.

9. Post-Closing: There may be agreed upon actions and conditions to occur after the closing – detail them in this section. Such agreements may include rights of sellers to check the books (if future payments are contingent upon future performance), remedies if payments are not made as expected, and required involvement (or lack thereof) by the seller or his or her management.

10. Risk of Loss: This section includes details as to who inherits the risk of loss prior to signing the agreement.

11. Attachments: Any support documents should be included here. Such information may include asset depreciation, financial statements and the like.

Supplemental Agreements

Covenant Not to Compete: Referenced in the purchase agreement, here the details of any agreements reached between buyer and seller regarding restrictions on the seller's right to open, work for or consult with a competitive business after the close are set out. This section should also include restrictions on the seller's right to disclose proprietary information or trade secrets of the business.

Consulting: As with the covenant not to compete, any consulting agreements between buyer and seller will have been referenced in the purchase agreement and are now detailed, including what duties will be performed, what compensation has been agreed upon and how long the relationship will last.

Promissory Note: If the purchase involved some sort of seller financing, there is likely to be a promissory note (a written document serving as legal evidence of a debt) to be signed. The note is often an attachment to the purchase agreement and includes how much the buyer is promising to pay and by when. Include language requiring written notice of default of claims and opportunity to remedy the problem before the loan is called. The buyer will want to be sure the agreement provides for a deduction of the amount due the seller if the seller defaults on the purchase agreement (this is called a setoff). The seller may require the buyer to purchase life insurance naming the seller as beneficiary.

Security: Also contingent upon seller financing, the security agreement details the agreement by the buyer to pledge business assets as collateral for repayment to the seller. The buyer will want to include only hard assets (not accounts receivable) and negotiate for the seller to agree to subordinate his or her security interest (so the buyer can get future bank loans if need be). The seller will want at least to be sure any subordination of interest is limited in size. Buyers will also want to include a clause (just as in the promissory note) making arrangements for notification before the loan is called and include a setoff. Any UCC-1 financing statements (which, as discussed, are security notices filed with the county recorder and/or secretary of state) agreed upon by both parties would be included with this attachment.

Employment Contracts: Whether contracts are with formal unions or informal collective bargaining units, if employment agreements exist, they need to be detailed and agreed upon by buyer and seller. If the seller has agreed to continue on as an employee of the new company, this agreement should be included (as should a consulting agreement) to ensure there are no misunderstandings.

Pension Plans: Maintaining and terminating pension plans can be a risky, complicated business. Include information on profit sharing plans, money purchase pension plans and defined benefit pension plans, as applicable.

Self-Funded Health Benefits: If such a plan exists, it could mean risks and complexities that should not be underestimated. Complete knowledge of responsibilities is absolutely necessary. Professional actuarial assessment and advice is warranted.

If the sale is a stock transfer, rather than an asset purchase, agreements of resignation from the seller and all corporate officers and directors at the closing, as well as representation of corporate good standing, would also be included.

Once the purchase and sale agreement has been negotiated and drafted to your satisfaction it is important to note that upon signing it there should be no looking back. You are either obligated to buy a business or sell a business. If the agreement hasn't been drafted to your satisfaction you are probably better off not signing it than hoping you can tweak or change a provision at the closing. (That said, consider our next case).

In general, you have a much better standing to negotiate when the agreement is still unsigned. Use that to your advantage.

Rich Dad's Tips

- Preparing a Purchase Agreement is not the time to test your paralegal skills. Careful drafting by an attorney is called for in this regard.

- As a buyer, make certain that no material changes to the business have or will occur. You don't want to open to your first day of business to any surprises.

- As a seller, if a promissory note and security agreement are involved, make sure that they are clearly drafted to reflect your understanding of the transaction. If payments are not made you will want these documents to protect you to the maximum extent possible.

When the agreement is signed, use that to your advantage to resist any last minute changes at ...

Chapter Fifteen

The Closing

The closing is the moment buyer and seller have been anticipating, the moment when ownership of the company is legally transferred from seller to buyer. If everything has gone smoothly and all parties (including hired experts) have done their work properly, the actual closing should be rather anticlimactic. The purchase agreement hammered out all the details; the closing is just ceremony.

The closing is usually at a law office – the buyer's attorney's, the bank's or the seller's attorney's. In attendance will likely be some combination of the following: buyer, seller, attorneys, buyer's banker, bank's counsel, seller's banker, business broker and creditors who have liens against assets. The bill of sale, consulting agreement, non-competition agreement, promissory note, security agreement and UCC-1 financing statements are signed. If the sale is a stock transfer, share certificates and officer and director resignations will be signed. Finally, the buyer endorses the check, or hands over a cashier's check representing guaranteed funds to the seller, in exchange for the keys.

A smooth closing can take less than an hour. However, if last-minute negotiations begin, everyone is in trouble. Many a closing has been bogged down or derailed by aggressive 11th hour negotiators. If the business brokers and attorneys have done their jobs, this should not happen. Still, sometimes it is impossible to prevent ...

Case No. 13 – Gorman, Larry and Ivan

Gorman owned King Gorman's Toys, a chain of four toy stores in a large metropolitan area. He had built the business up over the years and had developed enough of a loyal and local following that he was able to withstand the invasion of his turf by the Toys "R" Us and Walmarts of the world. Gorman knew his local market extremely well. Unlike Toys "R" Us and Walmart, he was able to stock his stores with the kinds of toys that truly appealed to his own market place. The stupid, the gross and the subtly offensive were left off the shelves. While the kids didn't really notice, the parents appreciated King Gorman's choices and retail philosophy.

Ivan was an aggressive retail executive with a significant amount of experience in distribution and marketing. He saw King Gorman's selection criteria and connection with parents as a benefit that could be successfully marketed in other communities. He was ready to put up a large amount of his own money and to personally guarantee an even larger amount of the bank's money to acquire King Gorman's toys and ultimately expand it into a four-state regional chain.

The purchase negotiations had been tense, emotional and at times, very bitter. Ivan was a hard charger who had to win on every point. Gorman was concerned about selling to someone who shared his business philosophy and couldn't imagine Ivan being that person. He had stormed out of negotiations on three occasions. At one impasse, the parties didn't speak for six weeks.

Gorman's business broker, Larry, had been the one keeping the whole deal together. Granted, with a five percent commission on a multi-million dollar deal, he stood to receive a very handsome payment if the sale went through. But, as many people involved in a number of such transactions will confirm, each deal develops a cast of unique players with their own defined roles within that particular deal. You'll have the aggressive one, the emotional one, the clueless one and so on. And, be it gossip or slander, the fact that everyone is talking to all the other players about each other helps to further shape out the stereotypes within that specific deal. And, interestingly enough, when the deal ends, everyone goes back to being their own normal selves until the next deal.

In this deal, Larry was the calm one, the mollifier. He was the one who brought the parties back together again. Larry accepted this role willingly, and not only for the reason that a wonderful payday was waiting at the end. Larry liked Gorman and appreciated his standards. He wanted to see the King come out okay after years of, in his own manner, serving the community. But Larry was also realistic. There were not many potential buyers willing to take on Toys "R" Us and Walmart. King Gorman's Toys was a tough sell and the perfect buyer was someone like Ivan, who had the experience, money and the supreme confidence to take on the world.

After eight months of negotiations and document preparation and refinement of documents and more negotiations, the cast of ten characters were all sitting in Gorman's attorney's large, wood paneled conference room with a stack of documents. Everyone held their breath as Ivan looked at the inventory adjustment schedule.

As in many sales of retail businesses, the exact inventory in King Gorman's four stores wasn't known until the closing time the day before the sale. If sales had been brisk in the days prior to closing, the inventory would obviously be reduced, and the buyer would then pay a little less for the business. So, it was important to get an accurate count before the closing, which they did, in an all-night, whirlwind count-a-thon at all four King Gorman's locations the night before. And, while some buyers and sellers will accept an inventory estimate for closing purposes, and some will set up a seller's escrow account with, for example, $10,000 in it, and pay the buyer out of it if need be based on a later inventory count being under a certain dollar amount, such flexibility was not a feature of this transaction. Ivan wanted to pay only for what he was precisely obtaining, and Gorman wanted nothing to do with him once he left his attorney's office that day.

In a demonstrative display of disgust before the other nine individuals in the room, Ivan threw down the inventory adjustment sheet. Gorman's face went flush with anger. Larry's heart sank, and the other characters all wondered what, at the 11th hour and 59th minute, was the problem.

Ivan complained that the inventory indicated that $50,000 worth of toys had sat on the shelves for over six months. He wouldn't buy old, dusty, outdated inventory. If it was over six months old, it would never sell, he said, and they all knew it.

What everyone at the table knew was that Ivan, true to his nature, was angling for one last price reduction in the final minute.

Gorman would have none of it. He was outraged and stormed out of the room. The cast of characters was shocked, except for Ivan, who displayed only a cold and smarmy smile.

Larry followed Gorman out of the room and caught him at the elevator. Larry tried to settle Gorman down by explaining that everyone knew he would pull this at the end. He allowed Gorman to vent his total distaste for Ivan. As he was calming him down, Larry began planting the seed that he could get Gorman the original sales price. Larry worked on the idea that Gorman wouldn't have to know how Larry did it, but that if Larry could get him the money that was previously agreed upon, with no $50,000 reduction, then they would have a deal. Gorman was still upset and venting but reluctantly agreed that under such terms they would have a deal. Larry said that Gorman wouldn't have to go back into the room, that he and Gorman's lawyer could handle everything, and that they would bring the papers over to his office for signature in a few hours. Larry again got Gorman to agree that if the original sales price was obtained, without any $50,000 reduction, or even a ten cent reduction, Gorman would sign the papers.

Gorman took the elevator downstairs. Larry went back into the conference room and put the deal together. It closed that same day.

How did Gorman get full price and Ivan get her $50,000 reduction? In the time-honored tradition of the broker reducing his commission to allow the deal to go through. Larry wasn't overjoyed about it, but cutting his $175,000 commission by $50,000 made perfect economic sense. If he didn't so agree, there would be no sale, and he would end up with nothing. There were no backup offers to purchase King Gorman's Toys and Larry didn't anticipate seeing any other offers at all. What particularly galled him was that he knew Ivan would pull this all along, he knew he had to have one last in-your-face victory, and he vowed one day to call the bluff on some obnoxiously aggressive buyer. But for now, Larry had $125,000 in his pocket and he was quite content to move on to the next deal.

The lesson of this case is that if one party has been aggressive and combative throughout the negotiations you might best be prepared for them to be that way at the closing. You and your attorney will want to prepare the purchase and sale agreement so as to box them in from trying to make changes. At some point, once all conditions have been met and the legal obligation to buy and sell has attached, you may need to call their bluff by saying no. These people are usually very egotistical so you may want to give them a way to save face as you deny their incredibly offensive last minute request.

Steps Prior to Closing

After the purchase agreement is signed, it may seem there is nothing left for the buyer to do but sign some papers. Wrong. Between the signing of the purchase agreement and the closing, the buyer (and his or her experts) will be busier than ever. Discussions about transition should take place; a corporation or LLC may need to be formed; new business forms (including business cards and stationery) will be ordered; principal customers and suppliers should be visited and any potential problems solved; and a meeting with key employees is recommended, as is a meeting with the landlord. Right before the close (a few days at the most), the buyer should go to the business and check assets and inventory for number and fixed assets for working ability. Buyers need to be sure that everything listed in the purchase agreement is present and accounted for.

If not already done, the buyer's attorney should make sure all contracts, leases and schedules provided by the seller are intact. And buyer and seller attorneys should meet for a pre-closing, during which all documents are reviewed.

Adjustments

Adjustments (also called prorations) are monies the buyer pays the seller for expenses the seller has incurred but which, due to the sale, benefit the buyer. Examples of adjustments include rent, security deposits, utility prepayments, premiums for transferable insurance policies and the like. Adjustments may mean more negotiations. The value of adjustments should be calculated by the attorneys for buyer and seller and are ideally made before the closing. A closing statement should detail the handling of all adjustments.

Checklists

When the buyer goes to the closing, he or she should have a list of all items to be picked up at that time. This should include:

- ownership papers for all assets purchased
- lease agreements
- customer lists
- business licenses
- transferable insurance policies
- keys to everything

Steps After Closing

If the business will be under a new name or a new address, the post office, telephone company and utilities companies will need to be notified.

Once the closing is accomplished and the business title is signed over, the purchase agreement no longer exists (except in reference to points that survive the closing). At this juncture, there is no more room for negotiations. Both parties have done all they can, and the deal is done. Neither party has any obligations other than those that are spelled out as surviving the closing in the purchase agreement. And any terms meant to survive the deal should have financial penalties or incentives to back them up.

Rich Dad's Tips

- Buyers should know their inventory levels before they close. Once you own the business the seller won't be there to reorder for you.

- Make sure to pick up everything – keys, codes, the works – at the closing. After closing, the seller may be unreachable in the South Pacific for awhile.

- It is important to remember that through surviving representations and warranties, as well as non compete and consulting agreements, that buyer and seller may be obligated to each other for a set period of time after closing.

You have either successfully bought a business or successfully sold a business ...

Chapter Sixteen

Moving Forward

It's done. You own a business. Maybe your first, maybe not. Either way, you have a lot of work ahead of you. A lot of work and a lot of potential for fulfillment, challenge and freedom. You hold the reigns. How far you go, how fast and in what style are all up to you.

Now that You're the Boss

You've spent months, maybe even years, in negotiations, searching out numbers, crunching those same numbers to see what would be best for you. Now, here you are staring at actual people, not numbers at all. Customers, employees and vendors are all relying on you, watching you, wondering how you will change their lives and livelihoods.

1. Customers: You will want customers to feel the same or better about the company under your ownership. This means putting in extra work in the beginning. Ask customers for feedback. Can sales methods be improved? If feedback comes to you as complaints, respond immediately and thoroughly, convincing customers of the fact you care. Do whatever it takes to rectify the situation and then follow up to be sure the customer is satisfied. Be sure all employees are doing the same and reward their good performance. If your employee selling techniques are rusty or out of sync with your style, consider retraining. If disagreements arise within the company, be

sure to keep the customers out of it. No matter what is happening behind the scenes, you want customers to see a smooth running operation that's main priority is to serve them.

2. Employees: You are now in charge of corporate policy. The best way to deal with the transitional period (and beyond) is to take the best of the existing policies (which, of course, you are intimately familiar with after your investigations) and discard what doesn't work, replacing it with something better. Employee morale is of the utmost importance during the transition. This is not the time to cut back on benefits to increase profits. Employees will already be feeling insecure. Short-term financial gains will not compensate for long-term losses when key personnel are leaving and/or hired away. Ideally, you have been working with a management team since before the purchase was finalized, so each member of that team is aware of their role in the transition and future of the company. They should know whether they will be staying or going and what compensation awaits.

3. Vendors: Relationships with vendors may have been fabulous under the old owner. In such a case, try to keep the transition as seamless as possible. Consider keeping the old owner around to help you get acquainted with vendors. Study the existing agreements and show you understand the details. If the relationships were strained, make the effort to show vendors how you are more reliable than the old owner. Meet with them, talk with them, go over the contract to see if better deals are available for either or both of you.

Choosing a Business Entity

In the case of an asset purchase, you will have a choice as to business entity: sole proprietorship, general partnership, limited partnership, S corporation, C corporation or limited liability company. Please do not choose a sole proprietorship or a general partnership. They feature unlimited liability for the claims of others, meaning you could be sued by a business creditor and lose all of your personal assets – your house, your bank account and the like – in the process. You are much better off with an entity that offers limited liability protection, a C or S corporation, a limited liability company or, with some structuring, a limited partnership. In choosing which of these entities to use be sure to consider such issues as taxation, ease of operation, management and control levels, ability to raise capital and ability to transfer ownership interests.

The issue of entity selection is a book unto itself. A good overview is found in *Start Own Your Own Corporation* by Garrett Sutton, which is part of the Rich Dad's Advisor series. Also, *How to Use Limited Liability Companies & Limited Partnerships* by Garrett Sutton deals with specific issues involving those entities. Furthermore, feel free to seek the advice of your attorney or CPA on which entity is best for you. And know that if a sole proprietorship or general partnership is suggested – you need a new professional advisor.

Business Redeployment Plan

If the previous owner prepared a business plan, you, as the new owner, should review and revise that plan forward for the next three to five years. If no business plan exists, you will want to prepare one for that same period of time. Business plans have been mentioned in this book in reference to getting money, and new owners may not think they need one because they're no longer looking for cash. It's easy to decide a business plan is too much work. Many new owners forego the hassle. However, many new owners go out of business as well. In part this is due to not following a well-defined plan of action. Don't be a failure statistic. The simple act of preparing a business plan can solidify and focus your plans for the enterprise in ways all the daydreaming in the world can't touch.

The business plan mapping your company's future is really a business redeployment plan. You are detailing how you are going to basically restart this business. Your plan should cover a general overview and key personnel, details as to how the business will create and maintain customers and financial projections. The SBA and SCORE are excellent resources for helping you create a business plan. Both offer free classes and free advice designed to help you do it yourself. Though you may wish to hire a business consultant to write the plan (expect to pay between $3,000 to $15,000), you should still be actively involved in its preparation. After all, if you don't know what's in there, it does you no good.

Business Credit

If you are a new entity or if the previous owner did not do so, you may also want to build up your business credit. This will help you avoid using your personal credit to finance your business. Building a business credit profile can take some time but it is definitely worth the effort. For more information visit www.businesscreditsuccess.com.

Making It Yours

Now that the company belongs to you, it's time to implement all those changes you saw in your head while negotiating the purchase of the business. Maybe you'll add new products or services. In many cases a new owner with a fresh vision is able to maximize the services or products offered. If you see a natural extension of existing products or services, do some market research and see what happens. If operational efficiencies are to be had you can now take the necessary steps to achieve them.

Perhaps you've had your eye on a new location since the first conversation with your business' old owner. Maybe it's a place with better foot traffic or lower overhead. Maybe it's just a nicer building or in a neighborhood more conducive to what you offer. Whatever the reasons, don't take the current location of your new business as the only option. And if you do decide the current location is fine, think about what you could do to spruce it up. Maybe an addition would help or a complete redesign of the interior. Maybe it just needs a fresh coat of paint and a redistribution of inventory. There are consultants who specialize in retail and office layouts. Or, you can do it yourself. Look at your space with new eyes and imagine the space completely empty. What would you do with it if you were moving into an empty building?

Do you really understand the competition? Your investigation into the business probably taught you more about the competition than the previous owner had even guessed at. Use this to leverage your position in the market.

Update business equipment where feasible. Bringing computers and other technology-based equipment up to date can pay for itself in no time through time savings alone. Just be sure that you only get what you need. Don't buy a cutting edge graphics package if you really only need word processing. Be current, but don't go overboard. Gadgets can be very tempting, but you are running a business, not engaging in a hobby.

Imagine no marketing had ever been done for your business. How would you do it? Marketing materials get outdated easily, sometimes simply because owners are used to them and take them for granted. Take the best of what exists, but bring your own spin to the materials, updating and upgrading them. Hire a PR or advertising firm to help with promotions if this is not your strong suit. Knowing the right message is only part of the battle. Knowing the right medium is just as important. Radio, TV, newspapers, billboards? You may need some advice on how to proceed. Get it, and start winning at marketing.

As always, with the right advice, you will start winning with your business.

Rich Dad's Tips

- Do not take customer satisfaction and employee morale for granted. Address the issues seriously and with concern, because during the transition they may have become problems without you noticing it.

- Consider preparing a brand new business plan for you brand new business. The focus of such a plan may be extremely valuable to you in starting out.

- Have fun – Be energetic. As Winston Churchill said: "Nothing great was ever achieved without enthusiasm."

Conclusion

As we have learned throughout this book, there are a number of pitfalls and obstacles to know and avoid when buying and selling a business. Being duly forewarned, as you now are, and with the help of your team of professional advisors, these issues can be dealt with properly and to your great advantage.

And, as we have mentioned throughout, putting together your professional team will be an important component of your success. Choose carefully and rely on your own intuition and inner judgment. Ask your friends and business associates for referrals. And then be sure to interview each professional to make sure you are comfortable with their experience, their fees and their ability and willingness to play on your team.

With the right team in place and the right preparation and precautions taken on your part you can and will succeed. With the right dedication and energy new business owners will provide for their future and their family's future. They will employ others and help their communities. It will be an exciting and rewarding journey.

Good luck.

Appendix A

Checklist of Information Needed in Acquiring a Business

1. **Business Information**
    Reasons business is for sale
    Amount of business for sale (all or part)
    History of business
    Description of products and/or services
    Address of business
    Date and state of incorporation
    States in which the company is qualified to do business
    Minute books, bylaws, certificate of incorporation, stock certificate book, and shareholders' agreements
    Shareholders' agreements
    Any special restrictions on the sale
    Shareholders and their holdings
    Rights of each class of stock and other securities
    Capitalization
    Fiscal year
    Accountants- for each: name, address
    Attorneys – for each: name, address
    Location of company records
    Credit rating
    Bank depositaries
    Bank references

2. **Operations**

Description of business, including manufacturing, distribution and marketing activities

Manufacturing history and agreements

Distribution history and agreements

Marketing history and agreements

Advertising history and agreements

Public relations history and agreements

Principal vendors and terms

Government contracts

Seasonal factors

Branch offices and associated operations

Subsidiaries, associated operations, and intercompany dealings

3. **Sales**

Description of the market

Relative size in the industry

Major competitors

Industry trends and recent developments

Industry advantages and disadvantages

Long range industry prospects

Client name and address

Number of customers

Principal customers

Customer continuity

Pricing policies and fluctuations in the past 4 years

Sales backlog

Sales materials

Sales personnel compensation

Effectiveness of advertising and other sales promotion programs

Gross and net sales for the past 5 years and for the last 12 months

Sales comparison with the industry for the past 5 years and for the past 12 months

4. **Personnel**

 Organization chart
 Number of employees and their positions
 Employee contracts
 Independent Contractor agreements
 Condition and accuracy of employee records
 Union contracts
 Morale and human resource issues
 Consultants – terms and payments
 Pension, profit sharing, insurance, stock bonus, deferred compensation, and severance plans
 Accident history, workers' compensation costs
 Industry comparison as to wage rates and number of employees

5. **Intellectual Property**

 Status of patents
 Status of trademarks
 Status of copyrights
 Status of trade secrets
 Status of domain names
 Use of name issues
 Intellectual property ownership – company or individual
 Licensing agreements
 Infringement and other intellectual property litigation
 Protection policies
 United States/other countries strategies
 Brand management strategies
 Research and development strategies

6. **Business Facilities**

 Location
 Status of leases
 Assignability of leases
 Land owned or leased – description, value, taxes, future plans
 Buildings owned or leased – description, value, taxes, future plans,

depreciation

Furniture, fixtures – description, value, condition, depreciation, useful life

Insurance coverage

Ownership of title

UCC-1 Financing Statements and other encumbrances

7. **Computer Systems**

Network system – type, setup

Computers networked – how many, description

Computers – condition, value, depreciation, owned or leased

Computer programs installed –leased or owned

Vendor and service arrangements

8. **Financial and Related Data**

Tax returns for the past five years

Annual and quarterly statements, including balance sheets, income statements

Earnings record, including gross and net profit margins

Earnings record compared to the industry

Break even analysis

Payroll-federal and state(s)

Annual and quarterly Payroll report

Sales Tax payments-proper filings

Nonrecurring income and expenses

Earnings forcast

Pro forma balance sheet

Chart of accounts

Cash and working capital requirements

Interest charges

Annual depreciation and capital additions

Inventory turnover and policies

Market and book value analysis

Accounts Payable and receivable analysis

Accounts Receivable

Notes payable and receivable analysis
Bad debts – collectibility and policies
Analysis of investments or other assets
Deferred expense analysis
Analysis of short term, long term debenture and mortgage debt
Existing and potential liens
Status of leases
Insurance coverage
Contingent liabilities
Status of any litigation
Status of licenses or franchises
Accounting procedures and practices
Review of all legal counsel opinion letters related to the business

9. **State and Federal Laws and Regulations**
   Current federal, state and local tax status
   Qualifications for doing business
   Good standing of corporate or other entity in all states
   Regulatory agency consents and issues
   Antitrust problems
   "Blue Sky" laws
   SEC filings and problems
   Stock exchange, if any, information
   Environmental issues (see Appendix B checklist)

10. **Comparison Analysis.** A buyer may want to compare certain target companies with those of similar companies for the past five years. Common ratio comparisons include:
    Earnings/book value
    Price/book value
    Price/earnings
    Price/fixed assets
    Sales/accounts receivable
    Sales/fixed assets

11. **Structure of Sale**

    Sale of corporate stock – unforeseen liabilities, taxation, corporate liquidation

    Sale of assets – purchase price, allocation, taxation, bulk sales laws, corporate liquidation

    Reorganization – mergers

12. **Acquisition Issues**

    Purchase price

    Purchase terms

    Financing

    Allocation of acquisition price

    Taxation issues

    Default issues and return of business considerations

    Brokerage fees

    Reasons for buying or selling

Appendix B

Checklist for Environmental Document Review

Environmental damage cleanup can be a staggering cost for the unsuspecting business buyer. What follows is a suggested, and by no means complete, checklist of records and documents relating to environmental concerns. These, and any other documents your professional advisors suggest, must be carefully reviewed before a business is purchased.

1. **General Information**

      Ownership and operational records

      Historical aerial and site photographs

      Plot plans, diagrams, schematics and building plans

      Indoor air quality reports

      Industrial hygiene/worker safety records and reports

      Any Phase I or more comprehensive environmental reports and surveys

2. **Hazardous Materials Management**

      Records and reports for spills/releases/incidents

      Hazardous materials inventory and storage plan

      Emergency response plan and training records

      Community and employee right-to-know records and training documentation

Local, state and federal government reporting requirements, including all reports to the EPA and related state authorities

Hazardous waste transportation and disposal records

Hazardous waste analysis plan and testing results

3. Air Emissions

Air permits and license/certificates

Regulatory compliance correspondence file and inspection reports

Reports on hydrocarbon storage systems

4. Water Quality

Water usage records

Water quality reports and records

Water system maintenance and repair records

Well water diagrams and reports

5. Waste and Storm Water

Waste and storm water discharge permits and ordinances

Diagrams of waste and storm water systems

Analytical testing records

Sludge disposal records

Regulatory compliance correspondence and reports

Local treatment plant correspondence and reports

6. **Polychlorinated Biphenyls (PCBs)**

> PCB reports to regulatory agencies
>
> PCB disposal and inspection records
>
> Electrical equipment with PCB inventory
>
> Reports and notifications of spills and releases
>
> Lab reports and correspondence

7. **Fuel and Oil Operations**

> Regulatory compliance correspondence and inspection reports
>
> Spill notification and reports
>
> Tank removal and closure records
>
> Inventory and usage records
>
> Maintenance and repair records
>
> Storage tank diagrams, specifications, and schematics
>
> Spill prevention and emergency plans

8. **Incinerators**

> Operating and inspection logs
>
> Operating permits and regulatory agency reports
>
> Specification and maintenance records
>
> All testing records

9. **Boiler and Heating Systems**

> Boiler operating permits and correspondence file
>
> Boiler inspection records and reports
>
> Heating system inspection records and reports
>
> Monitoring reports, records and charts

Appendix C

Letter of Intent for Sale of Corporate Assets

[DATE]

[NAME]
[ADDRESS]
[CITY, STATE, ZIP CODE]

Re: Purchaser of Assets of [CORPORATE NAME] ("Seller")

Dear [NAME]:

Over the past several months, [PURCHASER'S NAME] ("Purchaser") has worked in good faith with you, the Seller, to submit several offers to acquire certain assets and liabilities of [CORPORATE NAME] ("Seller").

This offer reflects our most recent discussion and is intended to conform with the terms under which we have been advised that the Seller's board of directors is prepared to accept this offer and to recommend it for approval to the Seller's shareholders.

The purpose of this letter is to outline the manner in which the Purchaser proposes to acquire from the Seller substantially all of the outstanding assets ("Assets") and certain liabilities of the Seller. The parties recognize that the transaction will require further documentation and approvals, including the preparation and approval of a formal agreement setting forth the terms and conditions of the proposed purchase ("Asset Purchase Agreement"); nevertheless, the Purchaser is executing this letter to evidence its intention to proceed in mutual good faith to complete work required to negotiate terms of a Asset Purchase Agreement that are consistent with this letter.

The proposed terms and conditions include, but are not limited to, the following:

Purchase of Assets: The Purchaser will purchase from the Seller all the assets, tangible and intangible, owned or used by Corporation in connection with its business as more fully set forth on Exhibit A hereto [ON EXHIBIT A, EITHER LIST ALL ASSETS, OR EXCEPTIONS TO ALL ASSETS, TO BE ACQUIRED] ("Assets").

Assumption of Liabilities: The Purchaser will assume certain liabilities of the Seller more fully described in Exhibit B hereto. The Purchaser will not assume any other liabilities or obligations of the Seller.

Indemnification: The Seller shall indemnify and hold harmless the Purchaser against each and every liability and obligation of the Seller other than those specifically assumed by the Purchaser.

Basic Price: $[AMOUNT], payable as follows: [DESCRIBE]. The fees and expenses of the Seller and its broker shall be deducted from the amount otherwise paid to the Seller and said fees and expenses shall be disbursed to the persons entitled thereto at the closing of the transactions contemplated herein ("Closing").

Adjustments: (a) The cash purchase price will be adjusted ("Adjustment") (up or down) to reflect the amount by which the values of the inventories on hand on the Closing Date exceed or fall below $[AMOUNT]. Inventories shall be valued at the wholesale price of such inventories on the Closing Date.

(b) Expenses, including but not limited to utilities, personal property taxes, rents, real property taxes, wages, vacation pay, payroll taxes and fringe benefits of employees of Seller, shall be prorated between Seller and Purchaser as of the close of business on the Closing Date, the proration to be made and paid, insofar as reasonably possible, on the Closing Date, with settlement of any remaining items to be made within 30 days following the Closing Date.

(c) If an Adjustment is made to the purchase price in the manner described above increasing or decreasing the purchase price, either the Purchaser or the Seller, as the case may be, shall deliver the amount owed upon the later of: (i) 30 days after the Closing Date, or (ii) within 10 days of the date that such amount is finally determined. In the event that such amount is not paid when due: (i) such amount shall begin bearing interest at the rate of 1% per month; and (ii) the party in default will pay the costs of the other party in collecting such increase, including but not limited to attorneys' fees and expenses.

Closing: The parties shall execute the Asset Purchase Agreement and Close the transactions contemplated herein on or before [DATE], subject to the extension contemplated by the section entitled "Exclusivity" herein.

Asset Purchase Agreement: The transaction will be subject to the negotiation and execution of a definitive Asset Purchase Agreement with terms satisfactory to the Seller and the Purchaser. The Asset Purchase Agreement will contain representations, warranties, covenants, conditions and indemnification provisions customary in transactions of this size and type and will provide for allocation of the Purchase Price among the Assets based on each Asset's agreed value.

Access: To permit the Purchaser to conduct its due diligence investigation, as long as this Letter of Intent remains in effect, the Seller will permit the Purchaser and its agents to have reasonable access to the premises in which the Seller conducts its business and to all of its books, records and personnel files and will furnish to Purchaser such financial data, operating data and other information as Purchaser shall reasonably request. The Purchaser agrees to retain all information so obtained from Seller on a confidential basis.

Upon the termination of this Letter of Intent for any reason, the Purchaser shall return promptly to the Seller all printed information received by the Purchaser from the Seller in connection with the proposed transaction.

Ordinary Course of Business: The parties agree that the Seller will be operated from the date hereof and through the Closing Date in the ordinary course of its business, consistent with past practices. Without limiting the foregoing, there shall be no change in accounting policies applied on a consistent basis and no accruals for payment of investment bankers or attorneys' fees with respect to the transaction for the Purchaser or the Seller. There shall not be any change or restrictions placed on the payment of ordinary course payments through the Closing Date. There shall not be any change in the method by which bonuses or other payments are made to officers and directors of the Seller.

Exclusivity: The parties agree to use their best efforts to enter into the Asset Purchase Agreement not later than [DATE] and the period beginning on the date of this letter and ending on such date shall be referred to herein as the "Exclusivity Period." The Purchaser shall have the right to request the consent of the Seller to a fifteen (15) day extension, and such consent shall not be unreasonably withheld. The parties agree that during the Exclusivity Period the Purchaser shall have the exclusive right to negotiate with the Seller for the purchase of the Assets, and during such Exclusivity Period the Seller agrees not to directly or through intermediaries solicit, entertain or otherwise discuss with any person any offers to purchase all or any portion of the Assets of the Seller out of its ordinary course of business.

Covenant Not to Compete: In the Asset Purchase Agreement, Seller, and each of its officers, directors and shareholders, both individually and as a group, will agree that they will not, directly or indirectly, through a subsidiary or otherwise, compete with the Seller in its business for a period of [NUMBER] years after the Closing Date. In consideration for this covenant, Purchaser will pay to Seller and such officers, directors and shareholders $[AMOUNT] which shall be divided among them as they shall so agree.

News Release: No party will issue or approve a news release or other announcement concerning the transaction without the prior approval of all parties as to the contents of the announcement and its release, which approval will not be unreasonably withheld.

Break Up Fee: Subject to the satisfactory completion of their due diligence investigation, the Purchaser expects to submit to the Seller within the Exclusivity Period a commercially reasonable Asset Purchase Agreement which reflects the terms described in this letter. In engaging in its diligence review, the Purchaser will expend substantial resources and incur substantial opportunity cost. Accordingly, to induce the Purchaser to enter into this Letter of Intent, the Seller agrees to reimburse the out-of-pocket expenses of the Purchaser if either: (i) the Seller fails to accept any commercially reasonable Asset Purchase Agreement which reflects the terms of this Letter of Intent and is offered by the Purchaser within the Exclusivity Period; or (ii) following execution of the Asset Purchase Agreement, the Seller fails to satisfy any of its obligations to deliver the documents required to close thereunder; provided, however, that under no circumstances shall the Seller be required to reimburse the Purchaser for its out-of-pocket expenses incurred in connection with this transaction in excess of $[AMOUNT]. The foregoing remedies shall be in addition to whatever other rights the Purchaser may have as a result of any breach of the Seller's obligations under this Letter of Intent.

Reimbursement of Expenses of Seller: In the event that all of the contingencies set forth herein have been satisfied of the Purchaser but the Purchaser is unable to sign the Asset Purchase Agreement or close the transaction due to the inability of the Purchaser to pay the purchase price in full, the Purchaser agrees to reimburse the Seller for all of its out-of-pocket expenses (up to a maximum of $[AMOUNT]) incurred in connection with the transactions contemplated herein.

Contingencies: This offer if contingent upon: (i) the completion by the Purchaser, to its satisfaction, of due diligence on the Seller, its markets, prospects and potential; (ii) satisfactory completion of legal due diligence, including review of material contracts and due diligence with respect to evaluation of potential liabilities related to [DESCRIBE] and tax matters; (iii) receipt of all required approvals, consents and authorizations of state and federal regulatory authorities; (iv) receipt of all required consents of third parties; (v) the occurrence of no material adverse change in the business or prospects of the Seller and its subsidiaries; and (vi) the completion of satisfactory legal documentation including adequate indemnifications and representations.

None of the parties hereto shall be under any obligation to any other party (except for the Exclusivity and Break-Up Fee provisions hereof) until a definitive Asset Purchase Agreement is executed.

This Letter of Intent may be executed in several counterparts and all so executed shall constitute one letter binding on all the parties hereto even though all the parties are not signatories to the original or the same counterpart.

If the foregoing is acceptable to you, kindly execute a copy of this letter in the place set forth below and return it (by facsimile [FAX #] or mail) to [NAME & ADDRESS].

Very truly yours,

_____

[PURCHASER'S NAME]

ACCEPTED AND AGREED TO:

[CORPORATE NAME]
a [STATE] corporation

by:_____
    [OFFICER'S NAME & TITLE]

Appendix D

Useful Websites

Corporate Direct – www.corporatedirect.com

Sutton Law Center – www.sutlaw.com

Internal Revenue Service – www.irs.gov

Small Business Administration – www.sba.gov

Service Corps of Retired Executives – www.score.org

Business Credit Success – www.businesscreditsuccess.com

Index

About the Author

Garrett Sutton, Esq., is the bestselling author of *Start Your Own Corporation, Run Your Own Corporation, The ABC's of Getting Out of Debt, Writing Winning Business Plans, Buying and Selling a Business* and *The Loopholes of Real Estate* in Robert Kiyosaki's Rich Dad's Advisors series. Garrett has over thirty years' experience in assisting individuals and business to determine their appropriate corporate structure, limit their liability, protect their  assets and advance their financial, personal and credit success goals.

Garrett and his law firm, Sutton Law Center, have offices in Reno, Nevada, Jackson Hole, Wyoming and Rocklin, California. The firm represents many corporations, limited liability companies, limited partnerships and individuals in their real estate and business-related law matters, including incorporations, contracts, and ongoing business-related legal advice. The firm continues to accept new clients.

Garrett is also the owner of Corporate Direct, which since 1988 has provided affordable asset protection and corporate formation services. He is the author of *How to Use Limited Liability Companies and Limited Partnerships*, which further educates readers on the proper use of entities. Along with credit expert Gerri Detweiler, Garrett also assists entrepreneurs build business credit. Please see businesscreditsuccess.com for more information.

Garrett attended Colorado College and the University of California at Berkeley, where he received a B.S. in Business Administration in 1975. He graduated with a J.D. in 1978 from Hastings College of Law, the University of California's law school in San Francisco. He practiced law in San Francisco and Washington, D.C. before moving to Reno and the proximity of Lake Tahoe.

Garrett is a member of the State Bar of Nevada, the State Bar of California, and the American Bar Association. He has written numerous professional articles and has served on the Publication Committee of the State Bar of Nevada. He has appeared in the *Wall Street Journal, The New York Times* and other publications.

Garrett enjoys speaking with entrepreneurs and real estate investors on the advantages of forming business entities. He is a frequent lecturer for small business groups as well as the Rich Dad's Advisors series.

Garrett serves on the boards of the American Baseball Foundation, located in Birmingham, Alabama, and the Sierra Kids Foundation and Nevada Museum of Art, both based in Reno.

For more information on Garrett Sutton and Sutton Law Center, please visit his Web sites at www.sutlaw.com, www.corporatedirect.com, and www.successdna.com.

How Can I Protect My Personal, Business and Real Estate Assets?

For information on forming corporations, limited liability companies and limited partnerships to protect your personal, business and real estate holdings in all 50 states visit the Corporate Direct website at

www.CorporateDirect.com

or

call toll-free: 1-800-600-1760

Mention this book and receive a discount on your basic formation fee.

Other Books by
Garrett Sutton, Esq.

Start Your Own Corporation
Why the Rich Own their Own Companies and Everyone Else Works for Them

Writing Winning Business Plans
How to Prepare a Business Plan that Investors Will Want to Read – and Invest In

Buying and Selling a Business
How You Can Win in the Business Quadrant

The ABCs of Getting Out of Debt
Turn Bad Debt into Good Debt and Bad Credit into Good Credit

Run Your Own Corporation
How to Legally Operate and Properly Maintain Your Company into the Future

The Loopholes of Real Estate
Secrets of Successful Real Estate Investing

• • • • • • • • • • • • •

How to Use Limited Liability Companies & Limited Partnerships
Getting the Most Out of Your Legal Structure
(a SuccessDNA book)

Bulletproof Your Corporation, Limited Liability Company and Limited Partnership
How to Raise and Maintain the Corporate Veil of Protection
(a Corporate Direct book)

Start a Business Toolbox
A Complete Resource for New Entrepreneurs
(a Corporate Direct book)

Best-Selling Books
in the Rich Dad Advisors Series

by Blair Singer

SalesDogs
You Don't Have to Be an Attack Dog to Explode Your Income

Team Code of Honor
The Secrets of Champions in Business and in Life

by Garrett Sutton, Esq.

Start Your Own Corporation
Why the Rich Own their Own Companies and Everyone Else Works for Them

Writing Winning Business Plans
How to Prepare a Business Plan that Investors will Want to Read – and Invest In

Buying and Selling a Business
How You Can Win in the Business Quadrant

The ABCs of Getting Out of Debt
Turn Bad Debt into Good Debt and Bad Credit into Good Credit

Run Your Own Corporation
How to Legally Operate and Properly Maintain Your Company into the Future

The Loopholes of Real Estate
Secrets of Successful Real Estate Investing

by Ken McElroy

The ABCs of Real Estate Investing
The Secrets of Finding Hidden Profits Most Investors Miss

The ABCs of Property Management
What You Need to Know to Maximize Your Money Now

The Advanced Guide to Real Estate Investing
How to Identify the Hottest Markets and Secure the Best Deals

by Tom Wheelwright

Tax-Free Wealth
*How to Build Massive Wealth by **Permanently** Lowering Your Taxes*